Way
Beyond
the Blue

The Memoirs of
Colonel Jackie Jackson,
USMCR, Retired

As Told To

LAINE BOYD

Way Beyond the Blue

The Memoirs of
Colonel Jackie Jackson,
USMCR, Retired
As Told To

LAINE BOYD

Cover photo: Colonel Jack Jackson flying a Harrier jump jet in front of the Missouri State Capitol building in Jefferson City, Missouri.

Publication, cover and interior design by

Marquee Publishing
3901 Berger Ave. • St. Louis, MO 63109
www.marqueepub.com • 314-202-2035

ISBN: 10: 978-0-9985017-8-9
13: 978-0998501789

Library of Congress Control Number: 2018945403

Published in the United States of America

Other Books By Laine Boyd

Unharmonious

Dinner and a Murder

He'll Find You: 'Til Death Do Us Part

He'll Find You: Final Justice

Coming Soon

Shakespeare's Directive

Dedication

To Arleen, Jacky, Kathy, and Jeff, with every ounce of my love.

And with the deepest gratitude possible to my beautiful Arleen, who made innumerable sacrifices to support me every step of our amazing partnership, way beyond the bounds of reason, for her understanding of my need to fly—as much as I loved those airplanes, they paled in comparison to you. I couldn't have done this without you; nor would I ever want to.

Acknowledgments

I would like to thank the following people without whose help and advice this book would not have been written: my publisher, Marquee Publishing, LLC, St. Louis, Missouri; Laine Boyd, the author, who spent well over two years working on this manuscript, and CaSondra Poulsen, editor. Each of these dedicated professionals provided support and encouragement, and I am truly grateful for their assistance and encouragement. Theirs was a labor of love and intense commitment.

I would also like to thank the following individuals who provided valuable input as test readers: Sandi Hafner, Renee Dyer, Gloria Harrison, Rick Rodriguez, and Lynn Meyers.

My friend, Ralph Conwill not only read the manuscript, but provided encouragement and a foreword.

I deeply appreciate the efforts and time spent by these dear individuals.

Foreword

Colonel Jack Jackson is a man with a list of accomplishments so long, it's dizzying. A decorated Marine who flew over six hundred-sixty combat missions in Vietnam. A test pilot for the Harrier Jump Jet. A man who has served his country all over the world as well as two-terms as Missouri State Representative. Colonel Jackson has piloted numerous and varied aircraft and flown donor organs to waiting recipients, or the families of wounded veterans to their loved one. He was instrumental in starting the Honor Flight, which takes veterans to Washington, D.C. to see their memorials. As a dedicated patriot, he has served his country in Homeland Security, numerous veterans committees, and in various aspects of the political arena.

Colonel Jackson married his high school sweetheart and together they have three children. In addition to his family devotion he also serves as a deacon at Fellowship of Wildwood Baptist Church, formerly First Baptist Church of Ellisville. To capture the life and heart of such a hero was daunting.

Anyone can put together a list of accomplishments, but Jack is so much more than the sum of his deeds. A Google search on Jack Jackson will provide pages and pages of facts about this humble hero. The list of medals, awards, accolades, and honors bestowed makes it hard to believe they are all wrapped up in one man. But Jack's character, integrity, heart, and attitude of humility outshine those. In writing this book, I wanted to present not a man with a trail of accolades, but the soul of a man who has lived a life of service to God, to his family, to others, and to his country, doing so with a humble heart, and maybe a practical joke or two.

I am certainly not the first, nor will I be the last person to say, "I remember the first time I met Jack Jackson." But I am the first to say what a privilege it has been to have been chosen to write the story of his inspiring and exciting life, and to get a glimpse into the heart and soul of a man who is a true American hero.

Several years ago, my husband and I were looking for a church. After a little internet research, we chose to visit a church not far from our home about which we'd heard many good things. After services that warm Sunday in June, we came home, and my dearly beloved plopped down on the couch, engrossed in a thrilling game of golf, while I changed into my raggedy shorts and a top that didn't match, to begin the Sunday chore of laundry.

I'd started the first load of laundry and moved on to bigger, dustier things when the doorbell rang. Where we live, in the middle of the woods, it's quite unusual to have an unexpected visitor show up at our door. I supposed it was someone who must have been lost—very lost if they'd made it as far as our place, and when I answered, I saw a well-dressed gentleman, holding a bag and wearing a bright, friendly smile.

"Hi, Mrs. Boyd? I'm Jack Jackson. You and your husband visited our church this morning. I'd like to thank you for your visit, and give you some cookies and a welcome packet!" He raised the gift bag in one hand and held out his other hand, still sporting an infectious grin. I shook his hand and invited him in. Goodbye golf match and hello to a couple dressed like they never held a job in their lives.

Jack made himself right at home, and after answering questions about his church, our ensuing conversation flowed seamlessly, as we laughed and talked about everything under the sun. What Jack thought would probably be a ten-minute visit, turned into well over an hour, which flew by, and when he stood and announced he'd taken enough of our time, we were sorry to see him leave. After only one visit by a total stranger, we felt we'd already made a friend. He was warm, friendly, genuine, and had a great sense of humor. Little did I know that someone so humble and down-to-earth would turn out to be one of the most fascinating people I would ever have the privilege of knowing, and that one day, I would be honored to write his life story.

As I embarked upon this journey of sharing the life of a man whose character seems bigger than life, I've spent countless hours asking him questions, listening to stories, and developing a warm friendship with Jack and his lovely wife, Arleen. They have become two of my favorite people on this planet, and my life has been deeply enriched for knowing them. A photograph of the entire Jackson clan hangs in my office, along with one of my most treasured photographs—Jack landing a Harrier jet in front of the Capitol Building. I get goose bumps just looking at it. Jack signed the photo for me, and it helped to serve as an inspiration as I undertook the writing of this book.

Jack has lived a life full of joy, sadness, excitement, danger, and faith. Within the pages of this book, I have tried to share his wit and wisdom through short stories that portray the experiences and teachings that shaped his noble character and have made him such a powerful influence in the lives of all who know him. And for those readers who do know him, yeah, yeah, yeah—he's also got a touch of smart-aleck behind the twinkle in his eyes.

The hardest part about writing this book was that Jack simply refuses to brag about himself. The book is missing photographs of his many medals, awards, and lists of outstanding achievements. Those who know him may think I have given him short shrift, but boasting is not in Jack's nature, and the book reflects those events and thoughts that Jack wanted to reflect. He passes off incredibly dangerous feats by saying things like, "Kids, don't try this at home;" or "That was a little dangerous." Yet this seemingly ordinary man, whose efforts and contributions have made the United States safer than it was when he got here, is most comfortable being known as Dad, Grandpa, and Husband. It is my hope that this book blesses all who read it as much as it has blessed me to write it. May we all embrace the joy, the courage, and the indomitable spirit Jack shares in his stories, and may we, like Jack, learn to soar *Way Beyond the Blue.*

~ Laine Boyd, Author

Foreword

Many of my earliest memories are of World War II military heroes. If not for them, we might be speaking German today. They were welcomed home as heroes, as they should have been, with ticker tape parades, marching bands, American flags flying, and above all, the respect of the entire nation. Jack Jackson's father was one of those who returned.

Many years later, in the early 1990s, Jack flew an AV-8B Harrier from St. Louis for delivery to the Italian military. My wife, Martha, and I were in Germany where I was involved in the reunification of East and West Germany, so the four of us met in Innsbruck, Austria to visit the place where Jack's father was shot in WWII on a road that connected Austria and Germany. It was a proud and emotional moment to stand in that place with Colonel Jackson, a Marine veteran pilot, and give thanks to God for his dad's homecoming following the defeat of Hitler's Germany.

We also gave thanks for Jack's return some three decades later, from Vietnam, where he served two tours. But during the period between WWII and Vietnam, many Americans had changed their attitude toward returning warriors who had fulfilled their pledge to follow the orders of the Commander in Chief. When then Captain Jackson landed stateside in his uniform, instead of a ticker tape parade, people yelled, cursed, and spat on him. But their despicable actions could not deter him from his achievements in military aviation, some of which are recorded in this book. I've learned a lot about pilots who are comfortable at Mach 2.0. I've also learned a lot about living and dying from my friend, Jack Jackson.

The people who assaulted this returning hero had no concept of the number of American lives Jack saved flying missions in both Huey helicopters and A-4 Skyhawk jet fighters. Neither could they know of his accomplishments as a chief test pilot for McDonnell Douglas in the development of airframes, controls, weaponry, and methods of engagement for the F-15, F-18, and the vertical takeoff and landing Harrier. If in the future America has to defend itself with the latest aeronautical technology, that technology will still reflect the influence of Colonel Jack "Action" Jackson pushing test flights to the limit and beyond.

Top Guns fly within the limits. Test pilots fly past the limits for two basic reasons: one is to prevent the pilot from killing himself, and the other is to prevent the pilot from making himself an easy target for the enemy.

A pilot can have the latest and greatest technology in the world available in the cockpit, but if the pilot is not the master of that technology, he or she will lose the plane and the battle. Technology is wasted if it is not mastered. Every time I flew with Jack, I *knew*—because I saw it in him, that he was not only the master of every instrument in the cockpit, he was the master of the sound of the engines, the flaps, the tires, all of it.

Even though I never flew in combat with Jack, I knew from watching him and experiencing his skills that in combat, Jack wasn't merely the pilot of the plane—he was the heart, soul, master, control center. He was the leader thinking ten miles in front of and behind the plane, ten thousand feet above and below, monitoring all the other aircraft around him as well as the weapons being fired from the ground. Flying isn't something that Jack did; it was who he was. That's why he was able to master the Harrier and teach the world that you actually can make a jet fighter bow and fly backward.

My wife and I have known the Jackson family for many years. We've spent countless hours together in the air, in church, raising children, and vacationing; even flying the F-18 flight simulator at McDonnell Douglas. It's an amazing digital machine with sound systems, wrap-around projection screens, and mechanical systems that make you feel like you really are in the air and that you *are* the pilot. It's thrilling. At the end of the flight, you have to land it. I thought I'd handled it well until I heard Jack's voice from the "tower" announce: "Congratulations. You are the first person to successfully land an F-18 two hundred feet below the deck."

Jack is living proof that Marine colonels have a sense of humor. It isn't like a normal sense of humor; it's a Marine colonel sense of humor. One memorable evening I was leading a Bible study at the church our families attended, First Baptist Church of Ellisville. The room was full of men and women. I was ten minutes into the program when Jack suddenly stood up and started walking toward me with the full swagger of a Marine officer (Picture Jack Nicholson in *A Few Good Men*). I knew I was in trouble. He came directly up to the podium and leaned toward me as if he were going to whisper something only I was to hear. Instead, he shouted in my ear: "Your fly is unzipped!"

Totally off-guard, I asked him, "Why did you do that?"

His reply was brief, to the point, and right on target: "Because you were the only one in the room who didn't know it!"

~Ralph Conwill, Friend

CHAPTER 1

Endings and Beginnings

What a beautiful day! I stood on the south lawn of the Missouri State Capitol Building, gazing with gratitude at a gorgeous blue sky. I inhaled deeply, intoxicated by the freedom my memories of flying through skies such as this one evoked.

I had cleaned out my office after finishing my second term as a Missouri State Representative and stood viewing the Capitol Building for the last time as an elected official. Captured by the clear and inviting azure above me, I soon became lost in a flood of memories. As a former Marine aviator and test pilot, I'd spent much of my life flying a myriad of different kinds of aircraft. The sky first called to me as a young adult, and like a moth is drawn to a flame, the invitation to flight burned within my spirit and blossomed into an exciting career soaring through the clouds.

I began to reminisce about my flying career, and soon my memories transported me back in time, as my mind drifted to one particularly exciting but disturbing event. I was testing an AV-8B Harrier, commonly referred to as the jump jet. When a test pilot begins to test an aircraft, he pushes the aircraft beyond that which it was designed to do so he can learn everything that it can and cannot do—in other words, to test the maximum limits of the plane's capabilities. The limitations within a plane's ability safely lie, are called the envelope. I was to begin a testing maneuver which went horribly wrong and turned into one of the most frightening and dangerous days of my life. Why, on this beautiful, clear day, my mind went back to this terrifying experience, I don't know, except that the memory of what could have been, had now crept into my thoughts.

My test team, the McDonnell Douglas Harrier Flight Test Team, was at Edwards Air Force Base in California, over the Mojave Desert, to test the AV-8B for departure and spin characteristics. Nothing seemed amiss as I climbed into the plane, strapped in, and secured my flight helmet. I took the plane to an altitude of forty thousand feet, with an airspeed of about .8 MACH, just under the speed of sound, to begin the test. I put the plane in a right turn, pulled back on the flight control stick to its full backstop, and pushed in full left rudder, which was opposite the turn. Rather than spinning, as it was supposed to do, the jet pitched nose down and cartwheeled, wing tip over wing tip, jerking wildly out of control. It snap-rolled to the left, which caused the controls to be neutralized and centered. This sudden, unexpected movement was so violent it threw me up against the top of the canopy, pinning me with such force, my flight helmet cracked, and in spite of being tightly buckled in, I was thrown around like a rag doll.

The jet then began to rock back and forth, while the nose was pitching up forty degrees, and then down sixty degrees, like a ball being slammed by an angry player at a pinball machine, only this machine was forty thousand feet above the earth. To keep the plane's only engine from burning up, I shut it down, and the plane dropped twenty thousand feet in about forty seconds. My stomach felt like it was in my throat, and I didn't understand what was happening. Confusion rendered me unable to process the issues with this plane. The controls in the cockpit were blurred, and the ones I could read, made no sense. My experience told me this was not a spin, yet I had never experienced anything like this before in any airplane, and I have spun a lot of airplanes. Whatever was happening was neither a spin nor an aero departure, and there was no communication from the team's testing monitors on the ground. Everything had gone eerily silent.

I had only a few seconds to act. I needed to stop the nose of the jet from pitching up and down immediately, and worry about the wings rocking back and forth later, or I was not going to come out of this alive. I pushed the stick full forward and held it there with all my might. After a couple more oscillations, the nose stopped, and then the wings stopped. By then, I had plummeted to nineteen thousand feet, and I needed to restart the engine, but what I did not realize during this frightening maneuver, was that the engine had sustained damage from the severe response to this test. If I failed to start the engine, I would have to eject, and the plane would be lost. Still falling without power, at fifteen thousand feet I attempted to start the engine. By God's grace, the engine roared to life. I breathed a heavy sigh of relief and sent up a silent prayer of thanks. However, unbeknownst to me, the damage to the engine resulted in a very hard landing, with the jet skidding off the runway and into a fence where it came to rest.

Meanwhile, back on the ground, the flight test director and the team of engineers monitoring my flight seemed unaware of my dire situation. As a matter of fact, they said nothing at all! I was amazed by their silence. They had to have seen what was happening on the monitors, but since I landed unharmed, and not needing fresh underwear, maybe they figured it was all in a day's work.

The jet sustained some damage, but in a few months, it was cleared to fly again. Because the aircraft looked like a leaf being tempest-tossed in all directions on a blustery day, this maneuver was named the Falling Leaf maneuver. It has never been attempted again, and was, in fact, considered so dangerous that the Falling Leaf maneuver is now prohibited in the pilots' handbook.

This same beautiful blue sky greeted me as I prepared to leave public service. I got into my car, looked at my lovely wife, Arleen, the sweetest gift God ever gave me, and said, "Sure is a pretty day!" She smiled, squeezed my hand, and reminded me of the many fun things we did on pretty days; picnics, long walks, sightseeing. As Arleen recounted the enjoyable activities she associated with pretty days, I began to reminisce as well, about where I had come from, where I had been, and how the chapters of my life had unfolded. Each person has their own unique story, some good, some bad; and the mile markers in the lives of every individual tell the who, what, where, and why of how their character developed; how they came to be who they are.

People often told me I was a breed apart. That description always humbled me, as it did not reflect my own opinion of myself. I simply lived my life as I believed God led me. While it's true that as we go through life, we are under a variety of authorities, the final authority that rules my life is the Bible. I believe its claim to be the Word of God is true, and although I've been under my parents' authority, my teachers' authority, employer and military authority, the ultimate authority is God Himself and His Word. The Bible says, "Delight thyself also in the LORD; and He shall give thee the desires of thine heart. Commit thy way unto the LORD; trust also in Him; and He shall bring it to pass." (Psalms 37:4-5, KJV). Although I've tried to live according to that verse, I've experienced many failures. I know I've disappointed God often. But in spite of myself, He surely gave me the joys of my heart.

God has designed a unique roadmap for each of His beloved children. Pulling away from the Capitol building that day, I reflected on mine.

Snippets and Snapshots

I was born in the small town of Sullivan, Indiana, an unpretentious farming community in the far western part of the state, in the heart of America. My parents, Ralph and Carmen Jackson, had grown up during the Great Depression, and like most of the country, they'd had to make do without a lot of basic necessities. My mother was raised in a dysfunctional home; her father, my grandfather, was an alcoholic. His enslavement to the bottle made life miserable for his family and was the reason for her early escape from their family farm.

My dad was raised on a neighboring farm. His parents were hard-working farmers working the poor ground of Jefferson County, Indiana. They helped to start the Indian Prairie Methodist Church, and every time the church doors were opened, my grandparents and their children were there. They were salt-of-the-earth folks who raised four children. My dad was the second. My mother and father had known each other since the fifth grade. When Dad was twenty, and Mom was only eighteen, they borrowed ten dollars to pay the preacher so they could get married. Life was not easy for them as young newlyweds, but with determined commitment and their deep faith in God, they remained happily married until death. The struggles they survived served as building blocks, cementing the love they had pledged.

I was born on November 13, 1942. My birth was difficult for my mother because I weighed almost eleven pounds. During her labor, the doctor told my father he would have to choose either his wife or his child, as both could not survive. My father, a man who valued life and whose faith ran deep, told the doctor he was not going to choose, that both had to survive. He would not lose my mother or me, and he didn't. We both survived, despite the doctor's warnings.

Shortly after my birth, my father took a job with an oil company in East Chicago, Indiana, and we lived on a small farm there. My parents believed that growing up on a farm was the best way to teach children a strong work ethic.

My mother had been a rebellious child to the point that when she was in the seventh grade, her mother told her she would suffer the consequences of her decisions because she wouldn't listen to anyone. She couldn't stand her father but loved the farming life. She enjoyed cooking for the thrashers when they came to work at harvest time.

In 1943, my father was drafted into the Army to fight in World War II. Like many young families during the era of the Greatest Generation, we moved from base to base until he left for Europe to fight the war. My father's story is worthy of its own book. There is far too much to tell to do it justice here. He was a man of integrity and faith, from whom I learned much and to whom I owe much.

While my father was deployed to Europe, my mother and I returned to Sullivan, Indiana, and stayed with my paternal grandparents. I was their first grandchild, and I grew close to my grandfather, who had become, at least for some time, the central male figure and role model in my young life.

One day, a man in uniform came to my grandparents' home with a telegram and asked to see my mother. The atmosphere was tense and grim as we learned that my father had been severely wounded, and was missing in action. My mother collapsed in a chair, devastated by the news. Grandpa exchanged a concerned look with Grandma, then scooped me up and took me out into the fields where we stayed for what seemed to me a very long time. I understood something bad had happened but at the age of only two, was much too young to comprehend the gravity of this situation. At that time, we had no television, certainly no internet, and my entire life revolved around my mother, my grandparents, and our simple life on a small Indiana farm.

After a long, difficult week, we learned that my father had been found alive in a field hospital, badly wounded, but he was coming home. Near the end of the war, he was in Northern Italy, when shrapnel from an enemy artillery shell hit him across the chest and face. It nearly took his life. The medics never removed all the shrapnel from him, and that shrapnel contributed to his death when he was eighty-two. It had lodged in his chest, across his lungs, which added to his breathing problems, because he had asthma as a child. It eventually moved to affect his heart, which caused it to fail.

The sacrifices that my father and countless others made in that conflict should never be forgotten. It was their dedication to our nation and the great flag that flies over it that inspired me when I became a young man to serve our country in whatever way I could.

When my father returned from the war, he took my mother and me and returned to his job in East Chicago, Indiana. Life was once again normal.

When I was four, my brother, Richard, was born, and when I was eleven, my youngest brother, Charles, was born. We called him Chuck. We, three boys, were all the children our parents would have.

We had livestock on our farm. As a youngster, I raised cattle. We had a milk cow, which I learned to despise. That cow *always* had to be milked. She didn't care whether it was raining, snowing, hot or cold, or if I had basketball practice. She just *had* to be milked. My father believed it was important for our cow to be milked by hand, morning and night. It seemed to me as though that stupid cow held a personal vendetta against me. No matter what I wanted to do or when, she had to be milked first. I had a pony to ride, however, and that eased the aggravation of having to milk the cow.

I loved horses—much more than cows. The freedom I felt when galloping on my pony, with the wind in my hair, bracing my face, was exhilarating, and horses are much more relational than cows, any day.

While we worked hard living on the farm, I have childhood memories that I will always treasure. Some of those happy memories include getting small gifts, like a baseball and a checker game for Christmas, planting a vegetable garden, caring for the other members of our livestock—not the cow, participating in 4-H, and playing baseball with my brother and the neighboring children. It was a simple time. My world was relatively peaceful. Technology and the invasion of all things digital had not taken over our lives, separating us from the company, companionship, and responsibilities of other people.

My brothers and I were quite fond of playing practical jokes on each other. One evening, when we were drinking Cokes straight from the glass bottle, my brother, Rich, and I shook our pop bottles, keeping our thumbs over the top, and letting a little bit of the fizz into our mouths. Chuck, the youngest, eagerly asked what we were doing. Little brothers love to tag along, and they are expert copy-cats. They also make great guinea pigs. We told him to put his thumb over the top of the bottle, shake it really hard, put it in his mouth and remove his thumb. Naturally, this resulted in Coca-Cola exploding out of his nose, his mouth, and I think, his ears, followed smartly by Coca-Cola spraying all over the ceiling, all over our living room, and soaking into the rug. Of course, this was hysterically funny. Rich and I howled with laughter until our mother came into the room, which promptly ended the laughter and commenced in a solid butt whipping. But some things are worth the pain, and the sight of Chuck being turned into a fountain of spewing Coca-Cola was one of those things.

As a youngster, I was interested in sports. Indiana winters are bitterly cold, and when the ponds froze, we'd play hockey with a stick and a tin can until someone would get hit with a stick or fall on the ice and get hurt. Then we'd all go home and return the next day to play again.

When I was a little older, I discovered basketball, but the winters in northern Indiana were so cold, we had to wear gloves to play on moonlit nights. We never took our gloves off unless we were losing the game because then it was easier to feel the ball with your hands. But if we were winning, we chose to keep our hands warm. Of course, we still had to do our chores, finish our homework, and milk that stupid cow before we could play. By that time, though, we were playing in the dark.

In the summer, all the neighborhood kids played baseball, until someone would hit the ball in the weeds and we couldn't find it. When I turned ten, Little League Baseball was organized in our neighborhood. I longed to play outfield, but because I didn't hit well, was left-handed and had a good arm, they made me pitch.

Besides baseball, we worked hard in the fields. While Indiana was cold in the winter, it was also hot in the summer, so we usually worked shirtless. The first few days, we would get so sunburned, it was unbearable. By summer's end, though, we were well-tanned.

I learned to swim when some older boys threw me into a pond, leaving me two choices: swim or drown.

When I was twelve, my father bought a .22 caliber rifle as a Christmas gift for me and taught me how to shoot. However, Dad didn't teach me about gun control. That, I learned from my grandfather. Grandpa had around ten grandchildren. He kept a loaded shotgun on the porch to keep foxes and raccoons out of his hen house. He firmly instructed all of his grandchildren that the shotgun was loaded and we must never touch it. All of his grandchildren obeyed him and learned to respect the meaning of a loaded gun—except me. He caught me holding the shotgun one day when I was on the porch by myself. That was the only spanking my grandfather ever gave me. Gun control took on a whole new meaning after that. So did the command, "Do as you are told."

On Sundays after church, we'd go to the home of my parents' friends, Mr. and Mrs. Olds, to make homemade ice cream. Dad would always start cranking the ice cream maker, and he would crank it hard and fast for about twenty minutes. Then he'd tell me to come over and take my turn cranking it. I would try with all my might to crank that handle, but it was so hard! I could *not* understand how my father had cranked it with such ease. Years later, I realized that since it's just liquid at the beginning, it was very easy, and the longer it turned, the harder it became. That was when Dad would let me take over the duties. We used to laugh together, remembering that joke he played on me. I thought he was so strong and I was so weak. In fact, my father was strong in many ways, but not because of the ice cream cranking. Family time on Sunday afternoons was full of love and laughter, and will always be one of my most cherished memories.

My youth was much like that of many young men of that era. We went to church on Sunday morning and

Sunday night. For that matter, every time the church doors opened, we were there. Growing up in church was a way of life for our family. My parents were people of faith, who embraced a close relationship with the Lord. They instilled their faith in their children by modeling it in their lives. My social life, before starting school, was with the friends I made in church and in the neighborhood, and that was a good thing. The company a young person keeps helps to mold their behavior and their values.

However, I was not exactly a saint. As with all children wending their path to adulthood, I was not immune to hormonal changes. One time, when I was a teenager, I found an adult magazine. While not exactly understanding everything within its colorful pages, which I studied more than any homework assignment I ever had, I knew it was wrong to be looking at such a magazine, and when I closed the end cover, I wasn't exactly sure what I should do with it. A stroke of genius led me to hide it in the corn planter. What could be more perfect?

Saturday morning arrived, and not seeing my father at breakfast, I asked my mother where Dad was. She answered that he was outside, cleaning the corn planter, something I could not remember him ever having done in my entire life. I deemed it not in my best interest to go out there and figured it was a good time to clean my room.

When Dad came in for lunch, he had the magazine in his hand. He looked at Rich and me and asked, "Who does this belong to?"

Rich and I looked at each other and solemnly answered, "It belongs to Chuck." Chuck was three years old at the time.

Our mother sighed and did not say a word to us, but she turned to Dad and said, "Ralph. It only takes two hours to clean a corn planter. You've been out there four hours. What were you doing?" We never saw or heard about that magazine again!

Each summer, I spent two weeks with my grandparents in southern Indiana. I loved helping them out on their farm. One time, while Grandpa and I were baling hay in the field, Grandpa laughed and said, "Why don't you get out of the hot sun and work up in the hayloft? When I get the bales, I'll lift them up to you." I thought that sounded good until I got up in the hayloft where it was a hundred and twenty degrees with no breeze. He sent the bales to me from the hay wagon, and I stacked them. Later that evening, when Grandma asked me what I had done, I told her I helped Grandpa load the hay wagons in the field, and then he let me get out of the hot sun by working up in the hayloft. I remember vividly, my grandmother turning to my grandfather and scolding him. "Carl! I do not want my grandson to ever work in the hayloft again."

He just laughed, "Okay, Mary." He tried to behave as though chagrined but didn't quite pull it off. However, I never did work in the hayloft after that. Grandma had spoken.

Grandma would ring a large bell to call us in from the fields for dinner, the noon meal. She was a good cook, so we never needed to hear the bell twice. Everything Grandma made was delicious, and all of it had been homemade and homegrown. Breakfast was the best; eggs, ham, bacon, gravy, bread, and whatever fruit was in season. If I'd picked blackberries for her, we looked forward to my favorite—blackberry pie!

After dinner one day, I asked Grandpa if I could shoot at a tin can. We were supposed to go back to work in the fields after we ate, but Grandpa agreed to my request. He told me that after we knocked the can off the post, we'd have to go back in the field, as there was still a lot of work to do. Both of us shot at it several times, missing each time, when Grandma walked out of the house, picked up the rifle, promptly shot the tin can off the post, looked at us with her hand on her hip, and ordered, "Now, get back to work!"

One winter, my brother, Rich, and I had gotten new winter coats. My folks had spent extra money to buy leather that year. It had been a sacrifice for them to spend so much on us, but they felt it was worth it.

Rich and I were outside playing when we found a skunk caught in a trap. Poor little thing! We had to help it. We carefully removed the skunk and carried it about a quarter of a mile back to our house, where we laid it on the porch to recover. The unfortunate skunk lay dazed on the porch, not moving. We hollered, "Mom! Come out! We have a surprise for you!"

My mother, thinking her little angels had picked some flowers or made her a gift, came running to the door. To her horror, she saw our dazed little skunk lying on the back porch. She screamed, "Get it off the porch!" When I picked it up, she screamed again, "Don't touch it!" This contradictory discourse continued for four repetitions. When I finally picked up the skunk and carried it back to the field, it happily dashed away, leaving us all with a less than favorable aroma. Our brand new leather jackets had to be burned, and we were severely disciplined. The smell lingered on me for weeks. I received my very first Marine haircut because our heads had to be shaved. I learned the hard way the vital lesson that skunks, however cute, must be avoided.

That same winter, we got our first television, a black and white twelve-inch screen, the only kind available. Rich and I loved to watch a show called *Big Top Circus*. We had never been to a circus, and were glued to the television in starry-eyed fascination at all the circus had to offer. We watched spellbound, as acrobats would jump on teeter-totters and send their fellow acrobats high into the air, landing on the shoulders of their partner. Rich and I watched all these antics, enthralled by the lure of the big top. We decided we could duplicate that act in our backyard. This would be fun! We got a board and several concrete blocks to set it across. I stood my brother on one end of the board, and I climbed onto the roof.

About this time, my father happened to look out the window and saw what we were doing. He raced out of the house screaming at me not to jump—too late. I jumped off the roof of the house and landed on the board, sending my brother high into the air. I realized then, for the first time, that I liked to see things fly. Perhaps this was a precursor to my career as a pilot. My father raced across the yard, arms outstretched, catching my brother just before hitting the dirt, and they both crashed hard to the ground. What a great sight! My enthusiasm was temporarily dampened when once again, discipline landed on my backside.

Dad made it abundantly clear to Rich and me that neither of us were to be on the board as the other jumped from the roof of the house. We nodded that we understood, and Dad turned and went inside the house again. However, Dad, lacking specificity in his admonishment, failed to mention anything about either of us jumping off the roof with something else on the board. Looking for a suitable replacement, we chose a large concrete block in place of my brother. Climbing up on the roof, with Rich watching the event this time, I leaped from the roof onto the board, just as my father, once again, raced from the house, screaming at me not to jump—too late—again. I sent the concrete block soaring high into the sky. As the song, says, what goes up, must come down, and the concrete block came down, crashing through the side window of our house. Stern discipline cured me of ever wanting to run away to join the circus. Soon after, a now-familiar phrase was coined: "Kids, don't try this at home."

My first day of school was unforgettable. I rode a school bus twelve miles one way to a public school in Dyer, Indiana. Due to overcrowding, I was bussed a half mile away from the school to a local church for first grade. That first day, the bus stopped at our driveway. My mother waved goodbye. Probably, the most exciting part of the first day of school was that I had my very own lunch in a sack. I had store-bought milk for the first time ever, and it was even chocolate!

One day, I missed the bus from the public school to the church. Uncertain of what to do, I walked home. The twelve-mile walk along a major highway took me all day, and I arrived home ten minutes before the evening school bus. My mother and dad didn't know whether to hug me or discipline me, so nothing was ever said or done. If a six-year-old child were to walk twelve miles home in the dangerous society we have now become, it would be a terrifying experience for the child and parents, but I never once felt in harm's way, walking home at a time when children had no reason to feel unsafe.

About that time, my dad got a promotion, and with the raise in pay, we were able to move into a nicer home. Because our family life was happy to begin with, I never even noticed that we had moved from a poor, struggling family to the middle class. It made no difference to us as a family, but my mother was happy to feel a little more secure.

During the fourth grade, my classmates learned my real name was Jackie and not Jack. That got me into a lot of fights on the playground. Some boy would tell me I had a girl's name. I would take a poke at him, and the ensuing playground scuffle would occur. Back then, the rule was if you got a spanking at school, you would get one at home as well. I got quite a few that year, usually two a day. I have since learned to appreciate the name Jackie; people remember it because it is different.

Also, when I was in the fourth grade, I had a beautiful black and white pinto mare that I loved to ride. Ginger was full of fire and spirit, and she loved to run. She was my favorite horse out of the four we owned, and we enjoyed a special relationship as we sped along, the wind against my face, lifting her mane, the next best thing to flying.

One afternoon, I was riding Ginger bareback, galloping across an open field, wearing a pair of low-cut tennis shoes. We were running fast when we came upon a gravel road. Ginger lost her footing and began to fall. I dove off of her, hoping to land clear of her, however, she fell on my leg. We both slid across the gravel road, and when we stopped, Ginger lay still on top of my leg. It hurt. My horse was dazed, but we both managed to get to our feet. My ankle was packed with gravel, which helped to slow the bleeding, and may have even saved my life. Ginger was severely skinned up and shaken, and my ankle hurt so much, I was not able to jump up on her to ride back home, so we had to walk back to the house. My dad saw us as we neared home, and called out to my mother. He took Ginger, to tend to her injuries, while my mother helped me inside to tend to mine. As soon as she saw my ankle, she announced that we were immediately going to the doctor. Like most children, I didn't want to go, but my pleas fell on deaf ears, so off we went.

The doctor was unable to get the gravel out of the wound, so he took a pair of forceps with cotton and swished it out. The pain was so intense, I passed out, and could not remember anything else.

Ginger recovered much more quickly than I did. For four months, I lay in bed with my foot propped up so it wouldn't turn over. The wound was open and so deep my parents feared I might bleed to death. Every night for six weeks, one of my parents stayed by my bedside to ensure that I did not roll over in my sleep and cause the wound to bleed. I missed the second half of the fourth grade and walked on crutches through the entire fifth grade school year. After eighteen months, I began to walk without a limp. I feel blessed not to have been permanently injured in this accident. However, the pain never dimmed my love of horses or riding.

Before I entered junior high school, my parents moved to a new home in a different school district. I dreaded changing schools to start junior high. The environment was difficult enough, without being the new kid in school, and having to make new friends. Making friends had never been difficult in my old school, but this was different. I was not on my own turf. I needed a best friend, but I never found one. I didn't know whether it was me, or that I was new to the school. I continued to work hard at my studies and was finally able to make friends through athletics. I played basketball and baseball, devoting all of my spare time trying to become proficient in these sports. In the eighth grade, I loved basketball. However, at five foot eight and one-half inches, I realized I would not play basketball at a higher level, so I turned my attention to baseball and football, as I entered high school.

My mother hoped that we would be musicians, but my feeble attempt at playing the trumpet as a seventh-grader in the Lincoln Junior High School band forced the music instructor to assign me the fifth chair when we only had three trumpeters.

High school was a refreshing change for me. There were many new faces from other neighboring counties, although, I began to struggle academically. It was difficult for me to maintain good grades. I went from an A-B student to a B-C student. As my frustration mounted in academics, I thought perhaps my career would be in athletics. This proved untrue. At the time, athletics consumed every aspect of my life. Later in life, I learned my high school was, itself, failing. The year after I graduated, the school was put on academic probation. I wished I had studied harder. I truly admire people who possess natural intelligence; however, I found that hard work and perseverance will always prevail, and I regret that I lagged in those areas.

Through four years of high school, I made friends. There were five particular friends with whom I carpooled so we could stay late after school and play sports. I dated a little in my junior year, but never went steady with anyone. I enjoyed the dances after football games, as well as the junior and senior proms.

I still loved to play jokes in high school. I guess that's something I have yet to outgrow. One time in the spring, after a baseball game, we had showered, and someone flipped me with a wet towel. Where I was struck is irrelevant. Suffice to say it was close to where I normally keep my wallet. Retaliation was first and foremost as I chased my assailant down the hall and flipped my towel to hit him. The towel missed my intended target and struck a fire alarm, setting it off. The baseball coach and the entire team explained to the local fire department that it was all a mistake. My assailant escaped punishment, but I was ordered to run fifty laps.

And then there was Chemistry—not my favorite subject. The chemistry teacher was boring—so boring I cannot even remember his name. The class was boring, too, but I sat next to my friend, Jack Wilson, who agreed that everything about chemistry was—you guessed it, boring. One day, Jack and I could take it no longer. While the teacher was droning on and on, *ad infinitum*, Jack and I began to open the drawers of our lab table. The drawers were filled with all kinds of fluids. We found a flask and began to pour a variety of the unknown liquids into the flask, just to see what might happen. It's not like we *planned* to blow up the chemistry room. The last liquid Jack poured into the flask resulted in a loud *WHOOSH*, and as he and I parted to avoid whatever we'd created, the room filled with thick smoke and the students cleared out fast. The teacher stood at the front of the classroom, speechless. He could only babble something that sounded like, uh, over and over. Jack and I thought it was quite a hoot, but the next person we saw was the principal, who arranged a meeting with what we called the board of education—a paddle. But again, some things are just worth it.

In high school, I was always the designated driver. I had no interest in alcohol, but a number of my friends did. Ted Stokes and Jeff Wilk got so stinkin' drunk one night, they could barely stand. I was driving Ted's car, and back then, the car seats were the bench type. I was going to take my friends home and pick up my own car, which was parked at Jeff's house. We'd learned in school that drinking alcohol kills brain cells. I have no doubt. As I drove, I listened to a conversation between my friends that clearly impressed upon me that many of their brain cells had been brutally murdered.

Ted asked, "Jeff, are you my buddy?"

Jeff said, "Yes."

Ted asked, "Can I throw up on you?"

Jeff replied, "Sure."

Ted, without missing a beat, proceeded to demonstrate a pictorial and smelly imitation of the eruption of Vesuvius that made me very grateful that the car I was driving was not my own.

I was involved in a number of school activities. I was a member of the senior class theater stage crew and also worked in a store stocking shelves. High school was a mixture of good and bad memories. The good memories are the friends I made. Unfortunately, as the years passed, I lost track of all of my high school friends.

I regret that I did not study very hard. This cost me dearly when I went to college. I didn't fully understand at that level, what it took to be a professional athlete, but I still dreamed that dream.

Not all of my youthful adventures were as exciting as temporarily defying gravity, ascertaining the extent to which Coca-Cola could explode within my little brother, or discovering the unpleasant side of skunks. Learning about life on a farm, as well as living not far from Chicago, Illinois, provided a diverse cultural blend and a solid basis from which to form basic values and a life philosophy. We'd drive to Chicago to see the history museums, and as a twelve-year-old, I'd hitchhike to Comisky Park to watch the White Sox play. My school, Lowell High, took field trips to the Planetarium, Museum of Natural History, Science Museum and others. I deeply appreciated learning the value of hard work, adopting a good work ethic, and the importance of fiscal responsibility, by raising our own food and not being ashamed to wear clothes with patches. These lessons helped develop the convictions on which lay the foundation for the values that I hold dear, and further instilled in me a deep desire to serve my country.

CHAPTER 2

College Life

Three days after high school graduation, and not knowing what else to do, I accepted a job at a steel mill in Gary, Indiana. After one week of working at the steel mill, I embraced a new perspective on obtaining a college education. If I did not go to college, I would be destined to spend the rest of my life toiling under huge, oppressive, hot steel rollers. The job was hot, dirty, and dangerous. My job was to take a shovel and pull the slag away from the rollers while tons of hot steel rolled above my head. One week of sweat-soaked drudgery and I was clamoring for another job, far away from the mill. For a high school graduate, the job paid well, but I really hated the work and didn't want to do this for the rest of my life.

Six weeks after accepting the job, I was thankfully laid off, and found another job with the Ford Motor Company, making car parts. Both of these jobs required me to join a union and pay dues. However, I received no union protection. There had to be another way.

I approached my father about attending college. My father was a quiet, intelligent man. This was the first man-to-man discussion we had. As we sat in the living room to talk, Mom got up and quietly left us alone, respecting our unspoken desire for privacy.

"Dad, I want to go to college."

He looked at me for a moment, and I noted a faint smile, an unconscious gesture he made when he was pleased.

"Son," he began, "Your grades are not adequate to attend college, but your SAT scores are very good.

You're a man, now, so I'm gonna give you a business proposition. I don't think I can give you the money to go to college, even though I have it. However, I will loan it to you at no interest, but the day after you graduate, you must pay it all back. Any course you fail will still be your debt."

I stared at him in amazement. I couldn't comprehend why he would have me borrow from him when he was capable of giving me the money to attend college. However, these were the only terms available to me.

"You got yourself a deal!"

At that time, I didn't understand the depth of his wisdom, but my father knew my emphasis was on sports, not academics. Although he loved me very much, he knew I'd never be a professional athlete. He knew that if it was my money I was spending, my chances of graduating from college with good grades increased. How right he was!

I applied to several colleges and was accepted to Purdue University. Because I struggled academically, I decided to attend a Purdue University extension campus near my home, which allowed me to save on room and board, as well as keep me focused on my studies.

Studying was difficult, and it took me some time to develop good study habits. I first majored in history, which continues to hold my interest, but still held onto my dream of becoming a professional baseball player.

Then one day, my college advisor told me I had to take a foreign language. I informed him that I wanted to study American history, not the history of a foreign country. I did not understand the reasoning behind a foreign language requirement. He looked at me and shook his head. I asked him which of the foreign languages he recommended, and he said, "Spanish." This proved to be my undoing as a history major.

Unaccustomed to the art of studying, I did not realize that a foreign language required study every day, without exception. I admire people who can speak and understand a foreign language, but I never quite got the hang of it. I'd been attending classes for three frustrating weeks when the instructor finally noticed me and called on me to answer a question.

"Mr. Jackson, what was the outstanding accomplishment of the Spaniards?"

The answer to his question lay buried somewhere in my Spanish-written textbook, which I was entirely unable to read. I stared at the instructor, while the rest of the class stared at me. Determined to set myself apart as a serious student of Spanish, I looked my instructor square in the eye and said, "I think the outstanding accomplishment of the Spaniards was that they learned the language." The class burst into laughter, followed shortly by the instructor's request that I leave his class. Thus, another of life's little lessons learned: A lot of people don't really care what I believe.

Not surprisingly, I next met with my advisor. When I informed him of the situation, he sighed and offered, "Perhaps you should transfer to the school of engineering or industrial management, since they do not require a foreign language."

I first chose the school of metallurgical engineering, since math and science were my strengths. One year later, it was apparent that metallurgical engineering was not to my liking. It wasn't that I couldn't pass the courses; I simply found the subject matter to be of no interest. I switched to industrial management and finally found my place in the academic arena of college. I thoroughly enjoyed these subjects, which ranged from mathematics to business law. At last, I'd made a choice that would serve me well for the rest of my life.

Academics were only one part of my life at college. I played baseball for Purdue for several years, and after a year and a half at the Purdue extension, I transferred to the main campus in West Lafayette, Indiana. By this time, I was at least somewhat older and wiser, and better understood the importance of studying. I also developed a deep respect for college athletes, as performing at a Division I level requires a tremendous amount of time and dedication.

As I continued to grow in knowledge and experience, I started to branch off into other areas to which I never dreamed I'd be drawn. I became involved in campus politics and was elected president of my dorm, which housed fifteen hundred men. I was elected to the campus-wide student body as vice-president. The university also held a mock national convention. I was elected president for this, hosting the delegates from various fraternities, sororities, and independent housing. I enjoyed those extracurricular activities and found my attraction to politics growing. I learned many new things about the political process and the way people thought and acted when involved in politics. This education served me well throughout life, even though, at the time, I never thought I would serve as an elected representative in a state office.

The emphasis in my college life began to evolve past athletics, and I enjoyed some of the fun and pranks that go with campus life. On one occasion, three of us traveled to the University of Illinois for a football game. One particular friend, Crazy Charlie, whose father was a fireman, had taken a tool from his father's fire department that opened fire hydrants. That evening, after the football game, which Purdue won, my friend snuck around the campus and opened all the fire hydrants. The spectacle was a sight to behold! Students were running through the water while the local fire authorities and police were searching frantically for the culprit. Needless to say, water was everywhere. Eventually, my friend was apprehended. As we stood by him, the Assistant Dean of Men said to all three of us, "I don't know who did this, but I'm asking the campus police to escort you three gentlemen off of our campus and one hour's drive out of town. From there, you may find your own way home." We were dropped off on a road in the middle of nowhere. It took us another five hours to walk and hitchhike back to our dormitory in Indiana, soaking wet.

Rivalries between fraternities and independents were ongoing, such as the annual snowball fight, which occurred at the first snowfall. Hundreds of young men gathered on both sides, throwing snowballs at one another. One side would charge, then the other. Once, the two groups joined in a unified effort. In the midst of the snowball fight, a campus police car arrived, lights flashing, in a feeble endeavor to stop the melee. As the police officers stopped the car, opening both doors to exit, all eyes of the combatants turned to them. Before they could so much as raise a hand, holler stop, or blow a whistle, snowballs from both sides bombarded them and nearly filled the car, since the doors were left open. The police car sped away, with both sides cheering victory. In hindsight, the two police officers were successful, because the snowball fight ended, and everyone returned home.

One of my more obnoxious pranks involved a particular fraternity, who had damaged one of the signs leading to the dormitory. I wish I could recall the name of the fraternity; it had a huge stone in front of their house with their Greek insignia chiseled on it. The stone weighed nearly a hundred and fifty pounds. One night, the independents removed the stone and sent it COD to a fictitious address in the state of Washington. When the stone was returned to the fraternity, a cash bill of over three hundred dollars was due for shipping and returning. That was a lot of money at that time, but no further property damage ensued.

My college years took place during a historic time in America. The age of innocence was ending, as the country moved toward the brink of turmoil and division. Lines were being drawn. They were hazy at first but became clear, as authority was questioned, long-held traditions overturned, and rebellion rising from college campuses divided friends and families. Every value and way of life that had been ingrained in the fabric of our democratic society was questioned and torn asunder, leaving in its wake a path of destruction bordering on anarchy. Confusion soon became the order of the day, with students making choices they did not fully understand, and for which they would suffer long-term consequences. The media, academia, and eventually, even some churches, were permeated with the angry, bloody feeding frenzy until innocence was lost, and America was no longer beautiful. I began college in one nation under God and finished in the same nation that now proclaimed His death.

It was a time to examine one's own values and conscience, to stand by a decision consistent with one's deeply held convictions. I was faced with such a decision during my senior year of college, as president of my dorm, during a weekend that Purdue was playing Notre Dame. Demonstrations against the war in Vietnam were beginning to escalate.

That Saturday morning, the campus "peace" demonstrators were holding a large rally outside of the administration building and asked me if I would be part of the rally. I wasn't too keen on them at that time, and even now, decades later, my feelings have not changed. But I told them we were the largest men's dorm on campus, and we would be involved in the demonstration. We made a huge sign about twenty feet long and ten feet high. Several hundred men escorted the sign to the campus. We were deliberately late because the other signs that read, *Ban the Bomb*, and, *Bring the Troops Home*, were already in place. I marched the men of my dorm to the middle of the demonstration amidst cheering everywhere. We unfurled our banner, proudly displaying a huge American flag with a sign next to it, proclaiming, *Beat Notre Dame*. The press was enthralled, the demonstration broke up and dismantled, and for some reason, my dorm was never bothered again by the peace movement.

Some things never change. There will always be people who demonstrate for peace, and people who want war, but no matter how we feel about the cause, whether it is just or unjust, it is imperative that we honor those who fight the wars.

The most significant life-changing event of my college years occurred over Christmas break of my sophomore year. My brother, Rich, was playing high school basketball, and he was quite good as a guard for his team. While home for Christmas break, I was watching him play in a tournament when suddenly my attention was diverted from the game to the most beautiful young woman I'd ever laid eyes on. She was like a mirage to a man dying in a dry desert. This vision of grace and beauty was a cheerleader for Rich's team. The basketball game was suddenly unimportant, and faded to background noise, as I spent the rest of the game watching her cheer, and trying to find someone who knew her name. No one knew anything about this lovely creature, cheering on the court. But I was determined to find out everything I could about her.

After the game, I asked my brother who the gorgeous cheerleader was. Rich knew immediately who I was talking about, but only laughed and said, "Her name is Arleen, and she's the most popular girl in school. She'd never even give *you* a second glance."

Well! That was all I needed to hear. My brothers and I always were, and still are, competitive. I looked at him with my chin jutted out, and said, "I bet I can get a date with her."

He took me up on it. "I'll bet you can't!"

"Oh yeah? What do you wanna bet?"

He replied, "I'll bet you a pizza."

I hoped he wasn't too hungry. If I did anything at all in my life, I was going to get a date with the incredibly lovely Arleen.

Two days later, Rich had a home game, so my golden opportunity was about to become a reality. After the game, I approached the beautiful goddess, Arleen. With a lump in my throat, I introduced myself and asked her if she would go on a date with me. It didn't occur to me that her parents might think that their high school daughter going on a date with a college man might present a problem. She stared at me in silence, which took, I think, half of my life, and finally said, "I don't think my parents will let me. But I'd like to go."

I asked, "Can I call you?"

She said I could, and after a couple of tries, Arleen and I went out on our first date on January 26, 1963. To this day, Rich *still* owes me a pizza! He brought a pizza to Arleen when I was in Vietnam, and Rich the ratfink considers that paying his bet. But the bet was with *me*, not Arleen!

Arleen graduated that May and planned to attend Ball State University in Muncie, Indiana while I still attended Purdue. I had no car, so I would hitchhike to see her on the weekends. She sometimes would ride with girls who were dating other guys at Purdue for events such as homecoming, football games, spring formals, and the like. During the summers, she worked, and I worked, but we always made time to be together.

While Arleen and I have now been married for more than fifty years, with three children and eight wonderful grandchildren, our romance was not as easy as we had hoped.

Arleen came from a fine family with several brothers and sisters. We soon found ourselves deeply in love, but problems arose over religious differences. Our families were deeply rooted in their faiths, but it was not a common faith.

As our relationship grew increasingly serious, the religious differences grew more prevalent under family pressure. Arleen and I had worked out the differences between our conflicting beliefs. Both families were of a Christian background, but the theological differences in our denominations grew to be divisive. Our families' bias of the other's religious convictions weighed heavily upon us and was at its height when we married. Her family refused to attend the wedding. Though my heart ached at their abandonment of her, I was proud of her on our wedding day, as she walked down the aisle alone, a stunning vision in white, and took my hand.

I graduated from college in June of 1966, with a BS in industrial management. Arleen had one semester left to obtain her teaching degree in elementary education. I had been searching for a job and was blessed to receive several interviews. I finally selected a position with General Motors Corporation in the town of Warren, Ohio.

I left Indiana and drove east to Warren, with everything I owned in the back seat of a just-purchased 1961 Oldsmobile. I rented a small apartment and entertained visions of becoming the next CEO of the General Motors Corporation.

Warren, Ohio, is a small town nestled in the northeast corner of Ohio, near Youngstown. I accepted a job as a sales engineer for the Packard Electric Division of General Motors. They manufactured the electrical wiring harnesses for all General Motors cars and trucks. I started the training program in June of 1966, availing myself of the opportunity to learn about each different department in the division, which included manufacturing, supply, accounting, quality control, and management techniques.

My desk sat at the end of huge rows of desks in a room about two hundred feet long and one hundred feet wide. There were over fifty desks in this large room, with upper management offices at the far end, each equipped with the luxury of a window and a door. I shared a phone with two fellow employees that we passed back and forth, depending on who answered the phone and to whom the call was directed. There were no computers on the floor. Several electric typewriters were available, but we were not allowed to use them because they were only for the secretaries, so we had to write things out.

Although this bleak picture of my new life may have seemed a boring existence, it was part of God's plan for our lives, which He would soon reveal. As I progressed in my career at General Motors, I began to travel with more experienced engineering teams to Detroit, Michigan, visiting the plants that made Buick, Cadillac, Oldsmobile, and Pontiac. I was amazed at how efficiently the General Motors automobiles were put together and how, in many cases, these factories could produce a car every minute. I was in awe of the modernization of the plants at that time, and even more, struck by the pride the workers showed in their product. There were a few union-versus-management issues, but there were bright, new shiny cars rolling off the assembly line, attesting to the value of teamwork.

I was living alone in Warren, Ohio because our wedding was planned for December, still several months away. I became involved with a church.

I met a gentleman named Robert Clark, a senior executive at General Motors, who helped change the course of my life. He and his wife, Anne, invited me to their home for dinner a couple of times. To my surprise, I soon realized that General Motors was not where I wanted to spend my professional career. Mr. Clark would talk about his career at General Motors. The more he talked, the less a career like that appealed to me. Although the company was good to me, and certainly a vibrant part of the nation's economy, I knew a life working in the automobile industry was not the career path the Lord was preparing me for. If I remained, I would never find fulfillment in this line of work, or consider my work meaningful. I believed the Lord had another plan for me, and I trusted that He would let me in on the secret in His good time.

Driving home from work one day, a sign grabbed my attention. *Join the Marines,* it urged. I pulled over to look at the sign, admiring the sharp uniforms of the United States Marine Corps, and I knew at that moment, I wanted to be a Marine. The next day, I walked into Mr. Clark's office and said, "Sir, I'm going to leave the company and join the Marine Corps."

Mr. Clark looked up at me and said, "Young man, would you like to fly airplanes?"

I responded, "No, sir, I don't want to be in the Air Force. I want to be a Marine. I really like their uniforms."

He began to laugh, and I started to feel a little unsure of myself. He said these words to me, which I will never forget. "Sit down, you knucklehead. I want to explain to you about Marine aviation."

Mr. Clark proceeded to tell me that the United State Marine Corps had pilots and airplanes. The pilots were trained by the United States Navy, and that he, himself, was a former Marine aviator.

This was the first time I'd ever considered flying, and needless to say, I was hooked. I went to the local recruiter, took the aviation skills test, and passed. On October 7, 1966, I raised my right hand and took the oath: "I do solemnly swear to uphold and defend the Constitution of the United States against all enemies, foreign and domestic . . ." I have never neglected my oath or broken my commitment. At the time, I wasn't sure what all this meant, but after flying in combat and hearing the last words of dying men who took that same oath, it is impossible to forget the power of those words and what it means to live in this great nation.

Overwhelmingly excited, I called my fiancée, Arleen, and told her what I had done. Arleen was surprised at my sudden change of career path, something she has since become used to. When I hung up, I believed she was proud of me, although the reality was that neither of us comprehended the full magnitude of what this meant, nor how it would change our lives forever.

Mr. Clark gave me excellent advice on what to do when I went to Officers Candidate School (OCS). One of the last things he said to me as I left General Motors was, "Just make sure your name tag is on straight." It wasn't until I got my commission that I fully understood what he meant.

Leaving General Motors was an interesting experience. I left the company for Christmas vacation and promised to return for my last days after the first of the year.

On December 30, 1966, Arleen and I were married.

Every wedding seems to have at least one unplanned but humorous moment. Ours was no exception. When the minister requested Arleen to place the wedding band on my finger, her bridesmaid, Carol Radu, dropped the ring. We could all hear the ring bouncing off the floor, and saw it rolling toward the piano. The youngest of my brothers, Charles, was thirteen at the time, and a member of the wedding party. He screamed at the top of his lungs, "I got it!" followed by his foot stomping on the ring, just before it would have rolled under the piano. He gallantly picked it up, handed it to Arleen, and announced in a voice loud enough to not require a microphone, "I don't think I bent it!" The entire church broke into laughter.

The reception that followed was a joyous gathering, for which I have my mother to thank for pulling it all together. Mom and Dad organized and paid for everything. Over three hundred friends and family attended our wedding celebration.

Eventually, time and understanding healed the divisive wounds surrounding our wedding, and we now enjoy a close relationship with both families. It's amazing what God's grace can do. One of the keys to a successful marriage is living a grace-filled life and standing ready to forgive.

We returned as Mr. and Mrs. Jack Jackson, to bid goodbye to our friends at General Motors, and to Warren, Ohio.

The senior executives at General Motors treated Arleen and me to dinner at their country club. It was a generous and supportive gesture, which we were excited to accept. Of the eight couples, most were in their mid-fifties, twenty to thirty-five years older than we were, and much more seasoned. While we were appreciative of such a grand send-off, we were somewhat uneasy in this environment, having never been to an elite country club before. I'd grown up on a farm, and Arleen grew up in a small town. We didn't do fancy dinners. During dinner, one of the vice president's wives sensed Arleen's discomfort, and in an attempt to make her feel more at ease, asked her if she liked the soup. Arleen replied, "Yes, very much. Would you like a bite?" She handed her spoon to the vice president's wife. Laughter broke out around the table. The lady smiled at Arleen, and kindly replied, "No thank you, dear," returning Arleen's spoon to her. We were a long way from Indiana farm country!

Bidding a fond farewell to all the kind people at General Motors, we returned to Indiana. Arleen had one semester of college to complete, half of which was class work, and the other half was student teaching. I dropped her off at Ball State for her remaining classroom work, gathered a few things and drove to Quantico, Virginia, to commence Officer Candidate School (OCS).

Our new life was on the horizon!

Jack and Arleen Jackson on their wedding day

CHAPTER 3

Boot Camp

January in Virginia was rainy and cold. I reported for duty at Officers Candidate School in January 1967. While I didn't know what to expect, I did know that I was definitely going to get my nametag on straight. I went from spending my time with a warm, loving wife to listening to the grating voice of a mean, domineering drill instructor. The next eleven weeks was spent in boot camp for officers. I was never called so many different names in my life as I was during those first few weeks as a Marine. I began to think my last name was *Maggot*, *Scumbag*, or a variety of other equally flattering epithets.

My ninety-cent haircut left nothing to the imagination. I certainly failed to get my money's worth. The barber put the clippers right between my eyebrows and went clear to my neck. It was over in about three minutes, leaving nothing but a few bumps and scars on the top of my head. I tried to stand in formation dressed in my newly-issued utilities, boots, and unstarched cover, which some people refer to as hats.

As I stood in formation with my fellow officer candidates, we were ordered to stare straight ahead. I didn't dare look around. One individual did glance elsewhere, incurring the wrath of a gunnery sergeant. We soon realized hell hath no fury like a gunnery sergeant disobeyed. I steadfastly refused to look side to side or move my head. There were fifty of us beginning OCS, and we looked terrible. Our clothing didn't fit. Some candidates were fat, some skinny, others short, and some tall. The only thing we had in common was fuzz for hair. Our first command was "Attention!" We were so green we had no clue at all what that even meant. In thirty seconds, however, we learned.

The primary purpose of OCS was to rid us of all our civilian habits, such as overeating, not exercising, and learning to take instruction without asking why. It is imperative that the men and women of the military take orders and execute them without question because in combat, there's no time to hold a meeting and take a vote on the appropriate action. You must trust your leadership and training. The leader is responsible for every person and piece of equipment in his command. I have never met a military leader who did not hurt deeply at the loss of someone in his command.

My first wake-up call was unforgettable. At 3:30 a.m., every light in our barracks was turned on. Two drill instructors stormed in, banging on trash cans, screaming at us to get up and stand at attention. I leaped from the lower rack of a bunk bed and stood beside it, not so much at attention, as observing the humorous scene of sleepy, clumsy candidates, feet tangled in sheets, falling out of beds, in an attempt to comply with a standard order at a ghastly hour. They were standing straight up, bumping their heads on the bunks above them, or, forgetting they were in the top bunk, falling out of bed and crashing on the floor. Language ensued that I shall not share, but you can imagine. It looked like the Keystone Candidates vs. Laurel and Hardy. Exercising extreme self-control, I managed not to laugh. Finally, standing at attention, the entire company was berated, told we were worthless, would never amount to anything, and we sure weren't going to be Marine officers. For some, unfortunately, that was true.

The first week included learning how to shine our boots. No matter how hard we tried, we couldn't get it right. The drill instructors never said we did a good job until the tenth week. They taught us how to starch our uniforms, salute, march and most of all, how to follow orders, never questioning the command.

We went everywhere as a unit. We were issued our weapon in the middle of the first week, the M-14 rifle. I memorized the serial number, and it became my best friend. I learned, *Every Marine is a rifleman.* I truly believed this even though my goal was to be a Marine aviator.

Classes commenced every morning at seven o'clock. We were out of bed at 4:30 a.m., dressed and ready in fifteen minutes, a sight to behold for fifty men using six sinks. Standing in formation, we marched to chow. We had twenty minutes to eat. A sergeant stood at the beginning of the chow line, telling us, "Take all you want, but eat all you take." There were no scraps. One pride of being a Marine was that the United States Marine Corps is responsible. They waste nothing.

After breakfast, it was off to the classroom. The subjects were not difficult: first aid, rifle instruction, including cleaning and firing our weapons, and basic tactics. We received a course in leadership and Marine Corps history. When classes finished, we ran back to the chow line for lunch, then out to the drill field, where we were taught how to march, the correct way to hold our rifles, various commands such as *present arms, right shoulder arms,* and *left shoulder arms.* We practiced, practiced, and practiced, until by the end of the program eleven weeks later, those of us who remained, mastered it with precision, as one unit.

The evenings were spent preparing for inspections. We had to make our beds, inspect our rifles and clean them, even though we had just cleaned them the morning before. We shined our boots, prepared our uniforms, and invariably, we would fall out of ranks, at which point, they made us run three to five miles. It felt like harassment, but in fact, they were getting us into the finest physical shape to endure the rigors of combat, in which we would be involved in only a few months.

The first half of basic training was the same program taught to the enlisted troops we were to command. It seemed there was no real difference between boot camp for enlisted and OCS, except we were not allowed to help our fellow officer candidates, should they encounter difficulties. For example, if we were on a forced march of twenty miles, and a fellow officer candidate dropped out of the march because of fatigue, we were not allowed to reach down and help our fellow Marine, whereas, in enlisted boot camp, everyone made it or no one made it. No one was left behind. The reasoning behind this difference was that it is hard to follow a leader you must carry on your back. This is interesting, because every Marine, regardless of rank, feels he is a leader, and the only ones you carry on your back are the wounded. No one quits. I believe this is true of all who serve in our military, not only the Marines. The character development instilled by being a Marine had deep and permanent roots, which built upon the foundation laid by my parents and my church. I could feel changes in my soul, as I continued to grow.

During the second half of OCS, we began to develop our combat skills. We ran tactical courses. We went to the rifle range, qualified, and learned the art of bayonet fighting. We practiced the tactics learned in the classroom out in the field. Mock battles were played out as each of us took a turn developing a maneuver or a strategy for every situation.

During this phase of our training, the drill instructors assumed a different role from their previous sadism. The same ogres who seemed to stop just short of torture had morphed into accomplished instructors. After each mock battle in the hills of Virginia, they took time to explain what we did right, and what we did wrong. Their valuable and detailed instructions were responsible for saving countless lives when we were deployed to Vietnam.

In spite of our hard work and rigorous training, military life was hardly devoid of humor. One evening after we'd been out in the rain and mud, we returned to the barracks soaking wet and tired, knowing there would be the usual shortage of hot water. I threw my dirty rifle into my locker and headed for a hot shower. Big mistake. When I returned from the shower, the others were cleaning their rifles, still soaking wet and dirty. I went to clean my rifle, and it was missing. I figured the drill sergeant had found it and taken it. My worst nightmare was about to become true. About thirty minutes later, the drill instructor called us to attention in the barracks. He sent a fellow Marine to his office to retrieve a dirty, filthy rifle. He screamed in a loud voice, "Candidate Jackson, front and center!" As I stood there staring at him and the rifle he held in his hand, he peppered me with questions. "What do you think of someone who would leave their weapon in this condition?" While I was staring, I noticed the serial number was not the same as my rifle. I was not certain where my rifle was, but the dirty weapon the drill sergeant held before me was not mine. I answered that the individual should do fifty push-ups.

He asked, "What else should happen to a person who leaves their weapon in this state?"

I replied, "They should have to clean everyone's rifle in the squad bay."

At this point, he handed me the rifle, and I said, "Gunnery Sergeant, this is not my weapon."

No laughter was heard in the squad bay, but deep breaths could be detected. He grabbed the weapon out of my hand and raced across the hall to an adjoining barracks. I sprinted down the stairs to his office and found my rifle sitting in the corner. I grabbed it and ran back up to my position and cleaned it beyond belief. Thinking I had won that battle, I allowed myself to entertain a fleeting feeling of smugness. But the gunnery sergeant had returned, and I was summoned to the front of the barracks again to present my weapon. The gunnery sergeant found a piece of lint on the barrel of the weapon and assigned me the esteemed duty of iceberg watch on the Potomac River.

It was the middle of March, around 6:30 p.m. I had my rifle on my shoulder, standing by myself on the bank of the Potomac, searching for icebergs floating down the river. A couple of hours later, a window opened in our barracks, out of which the gunnery sergeant screamed, "Have you seen any icebergs, you maggot?"

I said, "No, Gunnery Sergeant."

He replied, "Let me know when you see one." And he slammed the window.

About half an hour later, the window opened, and he screamed, "Have you seen any icebergs?"

I said, "Yes, I have." I thought I could get off this post and out of my punishment.

He asked, "What color was it?"

"It was white," I answered.

"I'm looking for a red one, you maggot!" he screamed and slammed the window shut.

Thirty minutes later, having learned my lesson, I was relieved of my post.

Another time, a friend of mine, Don, dropped some pennies onto the floor while we were doing manual of arms practice with our footlockers. Manual of arms practice is an exercise where the instructor says *Right shoulder arms*, or *Left shoulder arms*, or another command that tells us where to put our weapons. On this occasion, rather than our rifles, we used our large foot-lockers, so it was a very cumbersome exercise.

When we tried to pick the pennies up off the floor, the gunnery sergeant screamed at us that we were wasting the United States of America's money. We were told to hold the pennies against the concrete wall with our noses until we worked up enough sweat to make it stick. On a warm April day, we had on almost every piece of clothing, overcoats, field jackets, to the point that everything was sweating except our noses. Eventually, the pennies stuck to the post. When we left the barracks for the last time, three days later, they were still on the post, putting the Marine Corps' own twist on Benjamin Franklin's observation, *A penny saved is a penny earned.*

We were busy training all the time. In the quiet of the night, when I could finally be alone with my thoughts, my heart ached for Arleen, as the separation caused me to miss her so very much.

Finally, the eleven weeks passed, and so did I. The day we were commissioned second lieutenants was a proud day for me. Arleen flew in to pin my bars on my shoulder. I would have no one else but Arleen do this. I was looking forward with great anticipation to becoming a second lieutenant and starting my new adventure as a Marine officer. We had entered into an organization, a brotherhood, of which we would always be a member, and which would forever change our lives.

Although I have lost touch with the friends I made during those eleven weeks, I still remember their names. Should they call, I will be there for them. There was some sadness as well because out of the fifty who started, only thirty-six completed the training. I felt bad for those who did not. When someone left the program, nobody ever saw them leave. We only noticed that their bunk was empty. I would wonder, what happened? Some we knew, but others we had no idea. They desired that which we had just achieved.

I would never look down on them. The good Lord chooses different paths for different people.

In the auditorium that cold, blustery March day at Quantico, Virginia, we all stood, as the commanding officer swore us in. I remember saying, "I, Jackie Jackson, do solemnly swear to defend the Constitution of the United States of America against all enemies, both foreign and domestic…"

Once accomplished, a tradition in the Marine Corps dictates that you give a dollar to the first person who salutes you as a second lieutenant. By this time, we were all grateful to the drill sergeants who had shepherded us through the last eleven weeks. We got into formation. Having learned that both of our gunnery sergeants had been wounded in Vietnam, we, as a unit, went in together to buy each of them a sword. When they saluted us, we handed each gunnery sergeant not only a dollar from each of us but presented them each a sword. The expressions on their faces told us they were more proud of us than we were of ourselves. Arleen pinned on my bars, and I gave her a big hug. I was proud and relieved when those eleven grueling weeks were over, and hoped I would never be called scumbag or maggot again.

We spent the next four days on leave touring our nation's beautiful capitol, Washington, D.C.

The next order of business before leaving Quantico, Virginia and heading for Indiana was to purchase uniforms. It was quite a financial outlay, and I hadn't considered the total number of uniforms Marines were required to have. I thought I would only need a flight suit, because I was going to flight training in Pensacola, Florida. There's more, though, than the dress blue uniform of the Marines. There are dress white uniforms, green uniforms for winter, and khaki uniforms for summer. These can be worn with a jacket, tie, long sleeve shirt or short sleeves. I was also required to purchase a heavy, green wool overcoat, which I only wore the day I tried it on, as it was not needed in either Florida or Vietnam. Everything was perfectly fit and tailored. The most treasured item I was allowed to purchase was the officer's Wilkerson sword. Every sword is custom made to the purchaser's size. When holding the sword in my hand, with my arm fully extended, the tip of the blade came to my earlobe. Fifty years later, I still treasure that sword and take good care of it.

We loaded the car with uniforms and luggage that Arleen had brought for her trip to Quantico for our commissioning. We traveled westward to Indiana, to enjoy thirty days of leave, and then Arleen was to resume her student teaching.

On our trip home, Arleen gave me the wonderful news that I was going to be a father! I was thrilled at the announcement, but also concerned that the stress of military life while expecting a child and finishing college, might negatively impact her physical health. My concerns proved valid.

We were finally *Back Home in Indiana*. Arleen resumed her student teaching and would graduate in May. I enjoyed the rest but continued my physical training to stay in shape, as I prepared to begin flight training in Pensacola, Florida, as a naval aviator.

I left Indiana with all of our possessions and headed for Florida on May 1, 1967. Arleen would follow at the end of May after her graduation from Ball State University. Before her arrival, I had the task of finding a place for us to live in Pensacola, off the base. My three hundred dollar-a-month military salary severely limited the size and type of apartment we could afford. I found a relatively new efficiency apartment that fit our budget. It wasn't much; only two rooms, a sitting area, kitchenette, bedroom in the back, and a bathroom. Fortunately, it was furnished. The only two

pieces of furniture we bought our first year and a half
of marriage, were a baby crib and a high chair.

The money a Marine second lieutenant made at
that time would have qualified us for President Johnson's poverty program. But we were happy, and, like
many other young married couples in our situation,
we thought this was the standard. We had no com-
plaints. We had each other, the Lord, and our first
baby on the way.

Two months after moving into the little efficiency,
we heard that a small two-bedroom apartment had become available in our complex. It wasn't in our budget,
but we knew that God knew our needs. The owner of
the building allowed us to move into it for the same
price if we would help him clean it, which we were
happy to do. This was another way we could see the
Lord's hand in our lives. We needed more room with
a baby on the way, and all it cost us was a little elbow
grease.

I did manage to make a little time to play some
baseball for the U.S. Navy Flight Training Command.
Since I was left-handed, I pitched. Because the military moved all of us so quickly, I only played about
two-thirds of the season before I was moved.

During our time in Pensacola, our friends included
fellow second lieutenants and Navy ensigns in flight
training and their spouses. We joined the First Baptist
Church of Warrington and became involved in it. Our
Biblical convictions were the central role in determining our actions. I was grateful for a wife who shared
my faith and my convictions. They have served me
well all of my life, as I have strived to serve God.

I believe it is foolish to fly airplanes, whether in
combat or as a test pilot, without acknowledging the
reality of God, and knowing how to find His peace, the
peace that passes all understanding. To soar through
the air is to feel exhilarating freedom, the rush of your

heartbeat as your excitement crescendos to giddiness. But it can all come crashing down in an instant—wind shear, instrument failure, any number of things can go wrong. If you don't know the God who created you, and you don't have the peace that comes from knowing Jesus, that thrilling rush can turn to terror as you race toward your final heartbeat.

CHAPTER 4

Earning My Wings

Flight training began in June 1967. Becoming a naval aviator was a demanding experience requiring physical, intellectual, and emotional stability; qualities which I did not realize at the time I signed up were requisite. Our class started out as new second lieutenants with six weeks of academic schooling. I was a Marine, but there were many naval ensigns in flight training with me. Even though I was and always would be a Marine, if I graduated flight training, I would graduate as a naval aviator, because that was how Marine pilots were trained.

The six weeks of academics included aerodynamics, airplane engines, leadership and flight physiology. The class was all day, every day. Mid-term exams were only three weeks into our training and were the first point of stress. Failing a mid-term would result in the first round of individuals being cut from the program. Each stage of the training would leave fewer potential pilots to begin the following phase of training, and each successive phase of training was more strenuous. The following three weeks required us to double our efforts, as the program demanded even more study and time. The subjects themselves were not that hard, but we were being pushed to get through the flight program in a shortened time frame. The Vietnam War was heating up, and pilots were needed.

At the end of the last week, final examinations were administered, and more people eliminated. I was surprised at the number of aviation candidates cut from the program at this point because there was a shortage of pilots to fight the war. With the motto,

Shorten the time but don't lower the standards, we were pushed to our limits.

Once we completed the academic training, we quickly moved on to the physical portion of our training, which included running obstacle courses, swim qualifications, and land and sea survival training.

Having just completed OCS, I was in the best physical condition of my life, so running the obstacle courses was no problem for me. I could climb high walls, run a mile and a half on a sandy beach in flight boots in eighteen minutes, climb ropes, and do pull-ups and sit-ups. I completed these exercises with ease. Most of the remaining candidates passed this portion as well, but some who carried extra weight couldn't complete the course and were dropped from the program.

Next came swim qualifications. These almost washed me out of the program. I was at best an average swimmer. I didn't have much body fat, and the type of swimming we were required to do involved floating and maximum conservation of energy. The swim qualifications were by far, the most miserable of all the training. I suffered much pain and agony in this portion of the flight training and was significantly relieved when I passed.

Several training aids had to be successfully completed, and again, candidates continued to be eliminated if they couldn't pass the tests. The first training was with the Dilbert Dunker. This device was a simulated aircraft cockpit that was placed on a rail at a forty-five-degree angle. The end of the rail was submerged at the deep end of a swimming pool. I was placed in this training aid, strapped in as if I were strapped into the cockpit of an airplane. Then it was released, and I plummeted toward the pool. The device was turned upside down, simulating a crash landing. There I was submerged upside down, strapped in with no oxygen, except what was in my lungs when I hit the water. My task was to unstrap and bob to the top of the water without the aid of any additional oxygen or flotation equipment. I don't think there was a single person who went through the Dilbert Dunker training who did not complain about the amount of water that went up their noses.

The next exercise in the swim qualifications was the Parachute Drag. This simulated an over-the-water ejection and being dragged along the top of the water by a parachute. I stood with all my flight equipment on the edge of the pool with my back to the water, and my parachute fittings hooked up to a cable and a wench. Then, I was jerked backward into the pool. I had to release myself by the parachute fittings from the cable before I was dragged to the other end. If I didn't accomplish this promptly, I'd hit my head on the other end of the pool. The Parachute Drag was not as difficult as the other exercises, so I didn't sweat that one as much.

After the Parachute Drag, we were put in the deep end of the pool where a complete parachute was dropped over our heads. The flotation devices inflated so we could keep our heads above water. I considered this the most important water training because it taught how to get away from a parachute that had come down on top of me without becoming entangled in the lines and being dragged to the bottom of the ocean. Several naval aviators had drowned by not following this procedure properly, and I had no desire to be added to their ranks. I had to move slowly backward, pulling the parachute over my head in front of me. It was imperative that I did not cut the parachute lines, as this only created more lines that might entangle me like an octopus. If something entangled an arm or leg, I had to take the time to untangle it, rather than cut it. Of all my water training, I remember this exercise most vividly because we had been warned that several deaths had occurred when the procedure had not been properly followed.

In another exercise, we had to jump off of a tower, approximately twenty-five feet high, simulating abandoning ship. This was not too difficult because there was no flotation gear, only the flight suit and boots. We were required to cross our legs, fold our arms, and step off the edge, dropping twenty-five feet into the water. That was the easy part. The hard part was having to swim approximately twenty yards under water. Before we could come up, we had to splash our hands above our heads, simulating pushing burning oil and fire off the surface of the ocean before we could take a breath. This was not so challenging if one could swim underwater a long time.

The worst device used in training was the Helicopter Dunker. It involved a huge barrel, the size of a helicopter that seated eight people. The Helicopter Dunker simulated a helicopter crashing into the water. When helicopters crash in water, they immediately roll upside down. I was strapped into the training device, and when it hit the water and rolled upside down, I had to get out and swim to the top. I had to remain strapped in, while I was hanging upside down until it stopped moving. I never inflated my life vest while inside the helicopter. To do so would pin me to the top and prohibit my escape. Each candidate had to perform this exercise three times.

The first time the helicopter went in and rolled upside down, we were allowed to escape by any means possible, either through the door, the cockpit or the windows. The second time, all eight people had to exit through the door. This was a problem for me, as the guy who went out before me was over six feet tall, and weighed two hundred pounds. It was easy to become confused as to which direction to swim to reach the surface. We were taught to follow the bubbles because they always rise. However, when this individual reached the door, he panicked and froze, holding himself to the door, which prevented the rest of us from getting out. I tried pointing to him to go up by reaching around him with my hand, but it didn't work. I was running out of air and out of options, so finally, I just punched him in the middle of the back, and he turned loose and swam to the top. When I reached the top, I was a bright blue color from being short on air. The safety divers did not allow this individual to try the third maneuver, which was a blindfolded Helicopter Dunker, simulating the same crash at night. Needless to say, that was a scramble of every man for himself.

The next phase of the swim qualifications was the most difficult for me. We had to swim seventy-five meters wearing all of our flight equipment, which weighed about fifty pounds. We had to use three different strokes: the backstroke, butterfly, and the side stroke. We were disqualified if we touched the bottom or sides of the pool. When I reached the last ten meters of the swim, I thought I wasn't going to make it. One of the naval swim instructors hollered encouragement to me, "You can make it, Lieutenant! You're at the shallow end, and there are only ten meters to go." I remember thinking when you are five foot eight and wearing all this equipment, there is no such thing as a shallow end. Once I reached the end of this grueling exercise, I breathed a huge sigh of relief, grateful to have finished.

For the next exercise, we had to drown-proof by treading water for two minutes without using our hands, and holding them up out of the water for the instructor to see. At the end of two minutes, we were allowed to inflate our survival equipment, use our G-suit or other flotation devices to stay afloat. In that two-minute drill with my hands out of the water, my legs became extremely tired. I took a deep breath.

All I had to do was keep my hands out of the water, I kept repeating to myself. I raised my hands and let my head go under. When the buzzer rang at the end of the two minutes, one of the swim instructors reached down, grabbed me by the back of the neck, pulled me to the surface and told me, "You passed, Lieutenant, but I highly recommend, with your lack of swimming ability, that you never eject off the end of the ship, or you'll drown."

We also had to swim a mile in our flight suit and boots in the training pool. Swimming was a challenge for me to begin with, and with thirty other guys doing the same thing, I was always getting kicked. I could not allow myself to think of the mile and the finish; I just kept telling myself one more stroke, one more stroke. I was relieved when this exercise was over, too.

The final phase of the swim qualifications was sea survival training. Once the drill instructors were convinced we could swim, we were put on a large boat and taken out into the Gulf of Mexico. There was a rail on the back-end of the boat that extended over the water approximately fifteen feet and sat thirty feet above the water. We were individually hooked to this rail, as always, wearing *all* our flight equipment on this warm, sunny day in the Gulf of Mexico. Facing the front of the ship, we stepped backward off the back of the ship and sailed down the rail, plunging face first into the water, towed by the ship traveling at fifteen knots. The object was to roll over, get my face out of the water, unhook, inflate my one-man raft, and climb into it. This simulated an ejection over water while being dragged by your parachute. Accomplishing this meant I was set up for a rescue.

I was seasick from bobbing on the Gulf of Mexico for two nauseating hours. Those two hours felt more like two years. I thought being eaten by sharks might be better than lying there, seasick! I couldn't wait for the swim qualifications phase of training to be over. The two longest hours of my life were in front of me. If I could just get through them, then this portion of training would be in my rearview mirror, and I would avoid another round of cuts from the program.

Finally, I completed the swim qualifications and the physical fitness portion of flight training. I was required to complete refresher swim qualifications every four years, and it never got any easier. Those who did not make it were given remedial training in the areas in which they struggled. The United States Naval Training Command made every effort to see that each trainee graduated to naval aviator. Although the Navy made sure we were well-trained, I was grateful I never needed my swim training. The clear blue skies, not the water, were calling me, and the sky would be worth the rest of the torturous training.

The next phase of our training was escape and evasion over land. We were taken into the middle of the forest of the Florida panhandle and taught to forage for food. We were left for three days. On the last day, we were required to escape and evade the enemy, which in this case, were the instructors. Only two Marines successfully escaped. One of them was me and the other was Mack. I thought it was fruitless trying to hide from the instructors in daylight because they were going to find you, as any enemy would. The object was to run toward friendly lines and keep moving for the first eight hours, hiding only at night. Mack and I kept moving at a fast pace for over two hours. We reached the friendly camp, that is, the buses that would take us home. Everyone else was captured. The look on the instructor's face when we arrived at the friendly camp, told me they were not accustomed to their trainees evading capture.

Our instructor asked us, "How did you two get here?"

We replied, "We just kept running."

He grinned and said, "Good job!"

The last section of our training was the flight physiology training. This meant experiencing vertigo, lack of oxygen, and night vision. I found this training fascinating. We studied the eyes and the effects of white lights versus red lights. I learned that a pilot must always believe his instruments, check them often and learn to trust them, rather than depend on his senses or feelings, especially at night. When flying, your senses can deceive you, and make you think you're in a different position or going in a different direction from what your instruments tell you. But your instruments, not your senses, tell the truth. As I grew in my faith, I understood how the same principle applies to our lives. Just as the pilot must trust in his instruments and not his feelings to fly and land safely, so must a Christian trust his instrument, the Bible, and not his feelings, to grow in faith and have a safe landing, spiritually, especially at night, when all around him seems dark. Putting our faith in the right instruments makes the difference between reaching our destination safely or going off course, and possibly crashing. God can be trusted, no matter what circumstances or feelings dictate.

We performed practice ejection seat training, where we strapped into a seat on a large rail. When the ejection handle was pulled, it simulated the first phase of an ejection. We watched films that showed what to do afterward, how to release the fittings, and how to avoid power lines and trees. This proved invaluable years later, when, as a test pilot, I had to eject from an aircraft I was testing in 1979.

Finally, we were placed in a large vacuum chamber where the air was reduced to that of an altitude of twenty-six thousand feet. It demonstrated how to recognize the lack of oxygen, or hypoxia in a high-performance aircraft. Hypoxia occurs when the extremities begin to tingle. If this happens, the pilot has to remove his flight gloves, which protect his hands from fire, to see if his fingers are turning blue. If they are, it's because there is a lack of oxygen, and the blood is re-routed to feed the main organs. Thirty-seven seconds is all the time anyone has from the onset of hypoxia, before they are no longer able to think logically. Death will occur in less than ten minutes. I viewed a film in training, where pilots were taken to thirty thousand feet and told to remove their masks. Then they were told to write their names, and after that, they were told to play patty-cake. Their names looked like chicken-scratch, and when they thought they were playing patty-cake, they were actually slapping their own faces.

This completed the ground training required before the actual flying of the beginning trainer aircraft, the T34 Mentor. However, later I used this invaluable training throughout my military and test pilot career on several occasions. On one flight, I was at twenty-six thousand feet when the canopy of my Harrier started to open, causing the cockpit to depressurize. I slammed the canopy shut so it wouldn't come off, and went one hundred percent oxygen. I did a straight down-dive to below ten thousand feet, where the body normalizes.

The ground training was conducted at Naval Air Station or NAS Pensacola Mainside Base. The next step was our first flight training assignment near Pensacola, Florida, at NAS Soufley Field. I looked forward with great anticipation to finally flying a military airplane.

I attended flight training six to seven days a week. Half of my day was in the classroom learning the systems of the T34. The other half I was in the air. The first flight was in the backseat with an instructor in the

front seat. It was easy, of course, as the instructor did
all the work. All I did was ride; not too challenging. I
had never even been in an aircraft until my senior year
in college when I flew from Indiana to New York for a
job interview. My vast experience as a passenger had
thus far been accomplished with success.

My second flight, however, was an entirely different experience. I was in the front seat, and the instructor was in the back seat. I made the takeoff, with no
idea what to expect. I was certain my lack of ability to
fly this airplane was going to kill my instructor and
me. I thought if I dropped a wing, we would crash.

Shortly after takeoff, my instructor asked me
where I was from. I thought this guy must be nuts because we were about to die, and he was making small
talk. Being a good Marine officer, though, I answered,
"Indiana, sir."

"Is that farm country?" he inquired.

"Yes, sir."

"What do they raise up there?"

Now, I was really worried. I wondered if I was wit-
nessing signs of hypoxia. "Sir, they raise corn, beans,
cattle, hogs, and horses." Heck of a conversation, considering this would be our last.

He responded, "That's fine, Lieutenant, but we are
now over southern Florida in an airplane, and we raise
the landing gear."

Oops! In my excitement after takeoff, I had forgotten to raise the landing gear. This was quite a clever
method of instruction. I learned two important points
to keep in mind when flying: One, don't forget to raise
your landing gear. And more importantly, two, don't
ever, ever forget to put it down.

Learning to fly was heavily geared toward knowledge of procedures. I studied each procedure at
length and devoted my best efforts to understand
the systems. Each flight was graded. The first mark

on the grade sheet was of critical importance, head work. How did I think in the aircraft? It was necessary to know procedures, but procedures and technical knowledge alone did not produce a competent pilot. Being able to think and stay ahead of the aircraft were even more important. The title of Marine aviator was not merely a job to be performed. It was a calling that defined your very character.

I had four flights with the instructor, who said nothing as I demonstrated the startup, taxi, takeoff, and use of appropriate radio procedures. We flew to an outlying airport and made two practice landings and takeoffs. If I performed well, the instructor would say to make the landing a full stop. He would then get out of the airplane, and I would take off for my first solo flight, which included two takeoffs and landings.

I have been immersed in aviation since June 1967 to the writing of this book, but I remember my first solo flight as if it were yesterday. It was an unforgettable thrill. Once my landings were finished, I stopped, picked up my instructor and flew back to the main base. My first solo was celebrated that evening during happy hour at Soufley Field by cutting off the end of my military tie and presenting it to my instructor with a small gift. Thus, I began my career, flying by myself through some of the flight training.

In the primary phase of training, we learned how to fly loops, aileron rolls, and wingovers. This was great fun, a tremendous adrenaline rush, and I thoroughly enjoyed doing them every time. There's a freedom in flying that goes beyond the ability to simply control an aircraft. Winging through the open skies brings joy and exhilaration to the spirit, as you defy gravity and sense the presence of God.

At the completion of primary training, I went to intermediate flight training at NAS Whiting Field and began to fly the T28 Trojan. We learned formation flying, involving two and four plane formations. Every naval aviator learns these basic formations. Even the Blue Angels start at this point. We also began a new phase of training called instrument flying. Part of it was in an aircraft, seated in the back with a hood pulled over the canopy so you could not see outside the plane. The aircraft was flown on its instruments with a safety pilot in the front seat, and that pilot did the take-offs and landings. I felt contained in a small, dark world, trusting nothing but my training and the aircraft's instruments. I was glad that I was not claustrophobic, but because it was disorienting, some of the trainees washed out of the program because they failed to trust their instruments.

During this phase, I was introduced to simulators. Although simulators are sophisticated, and in many cases, come close to duplicating the aircraft, I have never found a simulator that acted exactly like an airplane.

During my original instrument training, I flew in a rudimentary simulator, which was nothing more than a windowless box with a few simulated instruments. We practiced instrument flying, including approaches to landing. One day, while flying an approach with the instructor, I didn't fly the approach very well. The instructor, a civil servant who was old enough to be my grandmother, opened the door and told me I just flew into the ground, and not to do that anymore. I re-flew the approach and made the same mistake. The instructor opened the door and stated in a gruff voice that I had hit the ground again. She instructed me not to do it again, and to re-fly the approach. I couldn't seem to get it right. I hit the ground on the third try, and this time, she opened the door of the box of the simulator and poured a handful of dirt down the front of my uniform and told me that this is what happens when you hit the ground. This was no cookie-baking granny! I never flew the simulator into the ground again after that.

During this training phase, we lost some of the candidates trying to earn their Navy Wings of Gold. This was the point at which those who were truly called to fly and blessed with natural ability were separated from those for whom flying was not destined. This was where I believed God had led me, and I worked hard to fulfill my calling.

While flight training involved hard work and concentration, there were still many funny moments to ease the stress. One time, Bob, a fellow student aviator forgot his call sign, and as he came around to land, he transmitted to the tower, "Tower, this is, uh…" A long silence followed. We were not permitted to land until we received clearance from the tower. As he got closer to the runway, his radio transmissions continued, "Tower, this is uh…" followed by more silence. Everyone knew he had forgotten his call sign. Finally, out of desperation, he screamed over the radio just prior to landing, "Tower, this is Bob, and I would like to land!"

The tower, an icon of dry understatement, calmly responded, "Well, Bob, you are cleared to land." It was a long time before we let poor Bob forget this, but none of us were immune to pulling stunts that resulted in taking our turns as the recipient of merciless ribbing. But as much as we enjoyed a good laugh, we always approached flying with the utmost seriousness and professionalism.

One of the highlights of my aviation career during this intermediate training was my first carrier landing. Prior to going to the ship, carrier landings were practiced on a normal runway. These practice carrier landings are called FCLP, which stands for Field Carrier Landing Practice. The maneuver is precise. The pilot must fly at a defined altitude, at a specific distance from the ship prior to landing, and be on final approach with little to no margin of error. For example, I had to be within five knots of my expected landing speed, and within one hundred feet of my glide path approaching the ship, while no more than three feet off the center line. I flew by myself during the practice approaches at the field. The Landing Signal Officer (LSO) stands next to a device on the ground, called a Fresnel lens. He will tell the pilot when he is not in the proper landing environment, but will say nothing if everything is correct.

My first carrier landing was aboard the *USS Roosevelt*. An instructor led three other students and me out to sea to the ship. The procedure was to fly down the side of the carrier from the back to the front of the ship on the right side. The altitude is usually six hundred feet, and we had to make a left-hand turn in front of the ship winding up abeam of the aft of the ship with the aircraft in its landing configuration, except we were not allowed to lower the arresting hook, which is used to stop the airplane. That is done from the cockpit. I made two approaches to the ship so the LSO could see how I did before he told me to lower my arresting hook. Then, I began the process of making my first arrested landing aboard a United States Naval Carrier.

There are four arresting cables, and the objective is to land on speed, on the center line with the arresting hook capturing the Number 3 cable. My first attempt went well. I flew the approach and made my first arrested landing, going to full power with the throttle, because if the hook misses the wire, breaks, or the cable snaps, the aircraft engine is already at full power. All I'd have to do then is simply go the missed approach, which means you go around and try again.

I landed at full power, awestruck at how big the ship was, once I was on it, compared to how small it looked from the air, and how busy it was. A sailor standing in front was waving at me and I waved back. I thought, what a friendly ship! He waved again, and I was impressed with the enthusiasm with which he greeted me.

In the midst of congratulating myself on my first successful landing, I heard a deep, resonant voice, yet could not tell from where it came. I saw no one and wondered if this was the voice of God speaking to me. It was not exactly what I expected to hear from Him. The voice said, "Pull the power to idle, Lieutenant. You are not going to drag my ship anywhere." Disappointed to realize that God's voice was, in fact, the ship's captain, I promptly complied. I had been aboard the ship at full power, and they couldn't get my aircraft unhooked from the cable. Someone behind me was trying to land. The friendly sailor who had been waving was trying to tell me to pull the power to idle, not welcome me.

I prepared for the launch that followed. What a ride! The aircraft was catapulted down the carrier deck, held back by a restraining cable. This is the only situation I know of in which we were allowed to salute a senior officer with our left hand. In this case, it was the catapult officer. When I was prepared to go, I didn't dare take my right hand off the stick, so I saluted with my left hand, and quickly placed it back on the throttle. Once the catapult officer saw that salute, he touched the deck with his hand, and the sailor on the side of the ship fired the catapult, launching my aircraft. Depending on the airplane, they can weigh anywhere from fifteen thousand to fifty-six thousand pounds, and go from zero to one hundred fifty miles an hour, and almost one-half the distance of a football field. I was airborne, flying a major weapons system, ready to defend my country. As a student aviator, this was the first time I felt I could live up to the slogan, *Heroes in Training.*

Once I had accomplished six carrier landings, I was considered carrier qualified as a student naval aviator. Flying back on the instructor's wing from the ship, where all four of the students had qualified, I felt prepared to defend our country in Vietnam.

On the heels of the most exciting accomplishment thus far in my aviation career, I was dealt a major let-down. At the time, however, I did not realize that my disappointment would turn out to be a blessing in disguise. I had been assigned to fly helicopters, rather than jets. My heart sank. I'd been told that if my grades were respectable and I flew good airplanes, I'd be given my choice of aircraft to fly. I wanted to fly jets. But, the cold hard facts dictated that the needs of the service took precedence over the wants of the pilot. In my case, and that of my fellow students, we were all sent to helicopters for advanced training.

I learned to fly the Bell Helicopter H13, which was similar to a traffic advisory helicopter, or small bubble aircraft. We learned to hover and practiced all the maneuvers we would use once we deployed to Vietnam.

I was glad to have Arleen with me during this important and exciting time. While she was the consummate supportive wife, a blessing for which I was and am thankful, as the training time went on, she did complain to me that all I ever talked about anymore was airplanes. I thought a minute and decided she was probably right. Okay, she was definitely right. Pilots can't talk about aircraft without using their hands to gesture while they talk, and I, too, had picked up that habit. If I'd been more graceful, I might have even looked like I was speaking in sign language. It was never my intention to make Arleen feel left out, or that she was less important to me than flying, so as the training time neared the end, I told her to meet me at the Officer's Club for lunch. I would devote some time just to spend with my wife over a nice meal, and we would not discuss planes, flying or anything except what she wanted to talk about.

When I got to the Officer's Club, Arleen was already there, talking with three of her friends. I watched her conversing and had to laugh to myself. There stood my beautiful wife, talking with her hands flying all over the place, exactly as I did.

At that time, Lyndon Johnson was the president, and he initiated a program called Johnson's Poverty Program. It didn't help in any way or do anything at all, but only stated that any household living on less than $300 a month was considered living under the poverty line. This was just the line of demarcation; it didn't mean the government provided any assistance, only that we were poor—something I didn't need the government to tell me. My income was $297 per month, so money was always tight. One day, I opened the mail, and there was a notice from the bank informing me that our account was overdrawn. I was always so careful; I didn't understand how this happened.

When Arleen came into the room, I told her "Honey, you're overdrawn."

She never missed a beat, and replied, "I am not overdrawn. You are under-deposited."

In June of the following year, my sweet wife, Arleen, proudly pinned my Navy Wings of Gold on my chest. From here, I received my orders to New River, North Carolina, to join my first tactical squadron, and begin my training in a combat aircraft before I left for Vietnam.

On the same day I received my wings, another trainee, John LeCave, received his wings, which his wife, Susan, also pinned on him. John and I served together in Vietnam. Arleen and I became close friends with John and Susan and remained so until John's death in October of 1997. However, we continue our friendship with Susan to this day.

Looking back at that time causes me to reflect on the changes in flight training. What took me eleven months now takes twenty-six months. When I received my wings several days after finishing flight training, there were only two of us—John and me. Today, they receive their wings in much larger groups. Times and training sure have changed since June of 1968.

CHAPTER 5

Bundle of Blessing

Arleen and I duly noted that couples who use the rhythm method of birth control are called parents. When we learned we were going to have a baby, we were thrilled, of course, but at the same time, I had mixed emotions. While children are a blessing, and one we looked forward to, having a pregnant wife, and months later, a baby, all while going through flight training, was also a distraction. I felt pulled in two directions at one time. God was going to bless us with a child, and I would need His strength to make it through training and fatherhood.

One night, Arleen and I went to the theater on base. Halfway through the movie, Arleen's feet began to hurt, so she took off her shoes and finished watching the show. When the movie was over, her feet were so swollen it was impossible to get them squeezed back into her shoes. She had to walk out of the theater barefoot and pregnant!

Our first child, Jacquelyn, whom we nicknamed Boo, and also called Jacky, was born while I was going through flight training.

Jacky's birth was not without complications, but as a new father, I had no idea what was normal, standard operating procedure, or what was cause for concern. Unlike pregnancy and childbirth today, fathers at that time were not well informed, and I was no exception. I was clueless as to what I should expect or when to worry.

The last two months of Arleen's pregnancy were difficult. She never felt well, but Arleen was a trooper and didn't complain. Looking back, she should have.

Arleen awoke at three o'clock in the morning with terrible pains. Nervous and unsure what to do, I called the hospital. They asked how far apart her contractions were. I timed them and told the nurse they were constant. The nurse urged me to get her to the hospital *now*. This surprised me because I didn't think Arleen had gone full term. By 3:30 a.m., we grabbed a hastily packed suitcase and headed for the hospital on the base. They immediately admitted Arleen and politely told me to go to the waiting room and wait. Sadly, fathers were not allowed at that time to be in the room with their wives for the birth of their own children. I'm so glad that's changed now. Fathers belong alongside the mother of their children; it just makes sense for the whole family.

I looked around the waiting room with a sinking feeling in the pit of my stomach, as the reality of fatherhood welled up within me. I cringed with dismay that my first child, my precious little girl, was going to be born in an old World War II barracks, which had been converted to a maternity ward. I imagined the hasty maternity ward accommodations were likely due to all the young lieutenants and their wives apparently using the rhythm method. I thought of the newer, modern hospitals, how their bright, shiny rooms would welcome a tiny new life into the world, yet my sweet wife and baby were relegated to a military barracks for such a momentous occasion.

Jacky was born about three and a half hours later, but there were complications. Our little daughter was healthy but weak. Arleen had developed toxemia and suffered the effects of that poisoning for two or three months after Jacky's birth.

Although having a wife and a new baby while going through flight training was a joyous blessing, it was also a full load to carry. We were grateful the Lord was our ever-present help, to carry and strengthen us, confirming that in spite of how we might feel, we were not alone. I'd come home from work and play with Jacky, ensuring that Arleen had some free time to herself. Arleen always got up with the baby for feedings, because I needed my rest to fly. We shared the workload as much as possible, including whenever little Jacky got sick. We were learning quickly the never-ending demands parenting entailed. But we grew together, and somewhere along the line, Arleen gave Jacky her nickname, Baby Boo.

Six days after my two best girls were settled at home, I was holding our daughter, when Arleen rose from her chair to walk into another room, momentarily lost her vision, and ran into the wall. We decided that Arleen should not carry the baby unless I was there to hold her arm and help her walk. She did not recuperate back to total health for three months after Jacky's birth. With Arleen requiring rest, we felt alone, without the benefit of parents or grandparents, as we tried to figure out the business of parenting.

The only new furniture we purchased that year was a baby crib and a high chair. Some dear friends, Jim and Patty Ferguson, had a son named Jimmy, who was about eight months older than Boo. Jim was going through flight training at the same time as I was. They were kind enough to give us Jimmy's baby clothes that he had outgrown. It was funny to see our beautiful little girl wearing hand-me-downs with *Jimmy* embroidered on them. We may have been poor as church mice, but we were happy and considered ourselves blessed beyond measure.

One evening, we were watching TV while baby Jacky was sleeping. The news was on, and we watched as women were burning their bras. It was quite a sight. I looked over at Arleen who was watching the scene with fascination, and asked her, "Why don't you get into that movement?"

Arleen wanted no part of it. "I am on a pedestal, and if you think I'm coming down to your level, you're nuts."

When Boo was about eight months old, she started pulling herself up on coffee tables and chairs and standing by herself. She never did crawl. One day, our landlord came to the door with two Chihuahua puppies. When I opened the door to welcome him, his two pups ran in as well. Boo, enthralled by the puppies, turned loose of the chair she was holding onto and walked across the room to pet them. Everything she did was cute, of course. She was the apple of my eye and had me wrapped around her little finger, which was also adorable. I was hooked on fatherhood. Boo is happily married now, with three children of her own, but I still call her my Boo.

Finally, flight training was complete. To say I was exhausted is akin to saying Niagara Falls has a little water in it. Arleen and I took Boo, put everything we owned in the back of a Pontiac LeMans, left Florida, and headed home to Indiana. I had thirty days leave prior to my new duty assignment at Marine Corps Air Station New River, North Carolina, in Jacksonville.

I learned something while I was on leave. At first, I was confused, but in time, I understood. My parents, who made absolutely certain while I was growing up, that I fully understood the meaning of the word no, were intent on spoiling my daughter. They apparently forgot that important word. For that matter, they seemed to forget that I even existed. They were wrapped around a tiny finger attached to a small, adorable human who could do no wrong. Ah, the joys of grandparenting! While Mom and Dad were spoiling our darling Boo, Arleen and I reveled in our thirty days of leave, especially the free babysitting. We felt like kids again.

In spite of the joy little Jacky brought, I noticed

that whenever I looked at my father, he bore an expression that troubled me. He knew I'd be deploying to Vietnam. A World War II veteran having served in combat as an Army infantryman and being severely wounded, Dad was well-acquainted with the face of war, the rigorous demands, and the life-changing effects. While I was yet untested in a foreign land, my father understood how combat changes a man forever, indelibly etching in the memory horrific scenes of violence and heartbreaking tragedy that tear the soul asunder. In his quiet, thoughtful mind, my father bade farewell to my time of innocence and trusted that the Lord would guard my body against harm, and my soul from the evil ravages of war. Dad did not burden me with his concerns. These thoughts he kept to himself, yet, it was impossible to keep the worry from his face.

CHAPTER 6

Final Preparations

We left Indiana, bidding farewell to many friends, including two special people, Rick and Sue Hunkizer, with whom we've remained close these many years. Sue had been Arleen's college roommate when they attended Ball State University, and Rick was my closest friend when I was at Purdue University. We introduced the two, and they were married shortly after our wedding. Rick joined the Air Force, and while I was in Vietnam, he was stationed stateside.

Rick told me thirty years after I had returned home, that he and Sue prayed for my safety every day. I was grateful for their prayers. I believe God answers all prayers. He answers either yes, no, or wait. In His mercy, He answered prayers for my safety with a yes. I imagine most families and friends of those in the armed forces pray for their loved ones' safety. Why some of those prayers are answered yes, and some answered no, I don't know. I do know, however, that God is sovereign. Isaiah tells us, "For my thoughts are not your thoughts, neither are your ways my ways, saith the LORD. For as the heavens are higher than the earth, so are my ways higher than your ways, and my thoughts than your thoughts." (Isa 55:8-9). God's ways are peace, but man's ways are war, and because the world is at war with God, He allows the natural course of that choice to follow. My finite mind cannot understand every question about God—especially the why questions, but there's an abundance of evidence to support a faith decision to follow Jesus, and I have never regretted making that decision. I know that God can be trusted in everything, small or large. He has already been to tomorrow.

Our leave was over, and our car fully loaded with all our worldly goods. Arleen, Boo, and I were in the front seat. Boo loved standing in the seat between us. Car seats were not required at that time, and though now, it would be unthinkable to travel without safely securing a small child, it was not an issue in the sixties. I remember Christmas of 1970; we'd gone back home to Indiana and Boo had assumed her usual position between Arleen and me. It had snowed. I hit a slick spot, and the car began to slide. Boo hung on to my neck while I held the wheel with my left hand and braced my daughter with my right. Fortunately, I got the car out of the skid, and as we continued to my folks' house, Boo grinned and said, "That was fun, Daddy! Let's do it again!"

We began the long journey to Jacksonville, North Carolina. Just before our arrival, we stopped for gas in Raleigh-Durham, North Carolina. It was a hot and humid June day. Our clothing stuck to our bodies, held fast by an everlasting supply of sweat. I asked the gas station attendant how much further it was to Jacksonville. He stood there a moment, pushed his hat back on his head, and in a good ole boy North Carolina drawl, thick with Southern roots, answered, "Ya drive as fur east as ya can until ya come to the edge of the swamp, and thirty-five miles further is Jacksonville, North Carolina."

Tears stung Arleen's eyes at the thought of living and raising our little Boo in such a desolate sounding place. A swamp was no place to raise a child. We followed the man's directions, and he was right. Jacksonville lay thirty-five miles past the edge of the swamp. We were a long way from the fresh-picked beauty of Indiana farm country.

I pulled into Marine Corps Air Station New River and checked into my tactical squadron. The first order of business was to find a place to live. I was a first lieutenant by this time, but too junior to be eligible for base housing. In addition, the administrative officer told me not to rent anything for longer than three months, because I would be in Vietnam by that time. I didn't mention that to Arleen, but it didn't take her long to figure it out anyway. Not much got past Arleen. She was as smart as she was beautiful and kind.

Just outside the base was an apartment complex, the Beecham Apartments. We rented a small, furnished two-bedroom apartment. It was a little more than we could afford, but the apartments were new and clean.

The first few days at my new squadron were spent checking in, registering the car for entry to the base, and updating Arleen's military ID. I located the Base Exchange and Commissary, and we began to look for a new church to attend.

I had to obtain my flight equipment for the aircraft I'd be flying. The camaraderie of the squadron was not as close as I'd anticipated. During this phase of the war, squadrons were not going over and coming back together, but on an individual basis. Once we completed sixty percent combat-ready training, we were all sent to Vietnam. The other forty percent would be learned during battle.

My first squadron was called VMO-1, and the aircraft making it up was a composite squadron of Helicopter Gunships and OV-10 Broncos. I was fortunate enough to qualify and fly both of them. The flight training was rigorous and thorough. Our instructors were captains and majors, most of them freshly returned from combat. What I learned from these people would be my best chance at staying alive. I didn't realize how much I enjoyed flying when I was in the training command because my only goal was to get my wings. Now that I was in a tactical squadron I had my wings and could enjoy learning to fly these two different aircraft.

The training started out in the UH-1E. The first eight to ten flights were nothing more than familiarization of flight—just learning to fly the aircraft; the approaches, flying instruments in case of inclement weather, and finally, the real reason you learned to fly combat helicopters and airplanes: tactics. The tactical training of the aircraft was by far the most important. One of the first things I learned was to always fly in pairs, that is, my wingman and me. In actual combat, there are four people in each helicopter, but for training purposes, there was only me, the instructor, and my wingman. I was taught how to fire the machine guns, shoot the rockets, watch out for my wingman, myself, the tactics the enemy were using, and what I needed to do when the shooting started.

Flying a tactical aircraft of any kind in any branch of service is an adrenaline rush like no other. I soon learned that the decision I made in an instant could mean life or death for me and/or my wingman. There was no margin for error. I learned from my training, and it was reaffirmed when I got into actual combat, that there will never be a substitute for the human mind on the battlefield for making instantaneous life or death decisions. Computers may help, but people win the war.

The other aircraft I had the privilege to fly briefly was the OV-10, which was used primarily to locate, observe and ensure ordnance (ammunition) was dropped on the enemy. It was a two-seat airplane. The pilot sat in front and an observer behind. The difficult part about that airplane was ensuring that I was always in a position from which I could spot the target and watch where the ordnance was to be dropped. Many times, I later learned, I was controlling the dropping of ordnance dangerously close to our troops. After about ninety days, my training was complete with both aircraft. Preparation for departure to Vietnam was full speed ahead. My sixty percent training stateside was complete.

Every person who has been in the military receives numerous vaccinations which the hospital corpsman administers. These shots presumably protected us from every possible illness, condition, or the onslaught of a myriad of attacks.

I also visited the dentist, who found a cavity. When he put in a temporary filling, I told him, "But I am leaving to go overseas in two weeks."

The dentist responded, "The temporary filling will be just fine, because if you don't come back, it'll be cheaper for the U.S. Government," and he sent me out the door. I walked out the door hoping it wouldn't fall out.

There was a social life of sorts in our new squadron family. It was one group, made up of two parts. One part had already been to war, and the other part was preparing to go to war. I didn't attend happy hour on Friday afternoons because I didn't drink. Alcohol has never held any interest for me. On one particular Friday, however, my commanding officer insisted that all of his pilots go to happy hour. He said it was an order. Unable to refuse an order, I complied but asked for a coke. My commanding officer, angry that I did not order alcohol, said, "You're not drinkin' a coke! I'm not gonna let you drink that." So I ordered a grape soda.

My commanding officer began to make fun of me because I respectfully declined to drink a beer with him. The more he picked on me, the more determined I was never to drink that beer. I had never tasted one before, and I wasn't going to start now. Abstaining from alcohol had never been a big deal for me; I simply wasn't interested. But the more he harangued me, the deeper I dug in my heels. My resolve angered him. I never said anything disrespectful, but the following Monday morning, I was scheduled to be the squadron duty officer three Sundays in a row, which was not a normal schedule. This duty was a twenty-four-hour watch during which I was responsible for the security of the squadron, ensuring that nothing abnormal happened in my area while everyone else was gone. I was disappointed to be scheduled three Sundays in a row, as Arleen and I were active in our church, and I did not wish to miss church.

A strange twist changed this. The first Sunday I was on duty, my squadron commander's boss, a full colonel, responsible for all the squadrons, came by late in the afternoon and asked how things were going. I reported, "Well."

The next Sunday, the same thing happened, only this time, the colonel asked me, "Lieutenant, weren't you here last Sunday?"

I answered, "Yes, sir."

He said, "I see on the duty roster that you're scheduled for next Sunday."

I said, "Yes, sir."

He looked at me with a frown, and asked, "Did you do something wrong?"

I told him what had occurred and why I was standing the duty. He listened to the entire story and never showed one iota of emotion. Marine colonels are good at that. However, when I returned to work the next day, my name had been removed from the duty roster. I never asked why, but I did wonder. I got my answer the following Sunday. Arleen and I were attending a local Baptist church off base. We dropped Boo off at the nursery and went in for the service. The colonel and his wife slid into the pew and sat next to us. He leaned over, smiled and said, "I thought it was time for you to be in church." 'Nuff said.

Most of the social events prior to my deployment to Vietnam were held in a senior officer's home, usually at the home of Major Gene and Vonette Bailey. They were always a lot of fun, and everyone attended. We talked about the Marine Corps, the war, and to a small extent, politics. The men would congregate around the drinks, and the women would gather between the dining room and the kitchen. Invariably, the discussions in both groups would be similar. The men would talk about their flying, and the women would talk about their families and children. Most of the children were babies.

The Marine Corps has a weight standard requirement that correlates with height. One evening at a social event, the major was chastising a captain for being overweight. He told him that he should get his weight down to one hundred sixty pounds, and he should have this accomplished in sixty days. As luck would have it, the overweight captain's wife walked by and overheard her husband informing the major that he didn't know how he could lose weight that quickly. His wife never broke stride as she walked through the room, put her hand on his shoulder, and announced, "Jerry, in sixty days, I am going to go to bed with a one hundred sixty-pound man. I hope you're eligible." A roar of laughter followed. Sixty days later, that officer weighed one hundred sixty pounds.

The short two and a half months from the time I received my wings until I departed for Vietnam, were enjoyable. I flew a lot. Arleen and I formed many wonderful friendships, which have lasted a lifetime. We learned what it meant to say, "Once a Marine, always a Marine." *Semper Fidelis* went from being a phrase to being a lifelong motto, as I began to understand its deeper meaning.

Arleen and I were shepherded by the more senior

officers and their wives. While they knew what we were about to go through, neither Arleen nor I had a clue. All we knew was that we were very busy. Training and preparations were one matter. War was another.

Reports of the war were on television every night, but at that time we didn't realize the extent to which the public, fueled by the media, held those who served in the military in disdain. Looking back, Arleen and I were very naïve. But we were not alone in our naiveté. Most of my fellow Marines had no idea how many American people were not behind us. I am deeply appreciative of the way the senior staff and officers sheltered us from the political arena and public opinion.

When I was fully combat-capable in my aircraft, I received orders to leave for Vietnam. Unlike today's military, where entire units are deployed as a group, we were given individual orders and sent over as soon as we were trained. A good friend of mine, Ken Pennington, who was one week ahead of me in my squadron in North Carolina, had already left.

We packed up everything we owned. I took thirty days leave, and Arleen, Jacky, and I headed for Crown Point, Indiana, where both of our families now lived. Rather than have Arleen stay with either of our parents, I rented a small home. It was old, but after a couple of coats of paint and scrubbing the floors, it would suffice for the next thirteen months. Arleen found a job teaching second grade at the Jane Ball Elementary School in Cedar Lake, Indiana. Between my parents and a good friend, we had babysitters for Jacky while Arleen was teaching.

There are two things no warrior, Marine, soldier, sailor, officer, or pilot, regardless of rank or military branch, ever forgets: the day they leave home to go to war, and the day they return. I was no exception. Even now, after all these years, I vividly remember Arleen's face as she drove me to the airport and walked me to the plane. Most military wives are strong individuals. My heart ached as I held my sweet Arleen, and she cried as I left. All the way down the jetway, I was thinking, I will come back! As we took off, a flood of other thoughts raced through my young mind as I departed for war this first exciting time. We dreamed of the glory and fame to be gained. We would be the next generation of brave warriors who would return heroes, like our fathers, who fought in World War II. Confident the battle was ours to be won, because this was right versus wrong, good against evil, and we would return from the battle victorious. Our training dictated that we were the Marines, we were the United States of America, and therefore, we were right. Victory was our only option.

Of course, everyone thinks they'll be a hero, but General George Patton said, "Your object is not to die for your country, but to make your enemy die for his."

I departed from Chicago, flew to San Francisco, and boarded a chartered TWA military flight. I had assumed we would go via military transportation. However, we were moving so many people so quickly back and forth, that charter airlines were necessary to get the job done. The route took us over Alaska, with a quick stop in Anchorage for fuel. The next landing was Da Nang, Vietnam.

The flight was exceedingly long. Discussions on the airplane at first revolved around the war, winning the war, and our families. Excitement ran high. Glory was on the horizon. But as the flight wore on, in the last few hours, the excitement turned to solemn, sober silence, and the talk turned to quiet reflection. Some of us would never return. Others would return broken, many beyond repair. It never occurred to us that whoever did return safe and sound would be changed for the rest of our lives.

CHAPTER 7

The Other Side of the World

The plane touched down in the late afternoon. Everyone on board strained to look out the windows to see this strange country called Vietnam. As we de-planed, extreme heat and humidity greeted us without mercy, announcing our arrival to the tropics. I broke into a sweat that soon dripped from me like rain. The air was thick and hot and caused our clothes to stick to us. Welcome to Vietnam. It would only get worse.

Before we even went through processing, we were shepherded to tents and shown where we could get a shower and some chow. Naturally, there was no hot water. The showers were crude with open ceilings to the sky. I found an empty cot in my tent. I would only be there one or two nights. Setting my sea bag and flight equipment on a small wooden pallet, I headed for a cold shower and some food.

Coming out of the chow line, I looked around and observed the scenery, trying to get a feel for this new land destined for destruction, a casualty of war. To the east lay the South China Sea, timeless and deceptively serene. Gentle, peaceful waves tickled the shoreline before returning to the deep. Over and over, their steady hypnotic rhythm beat, unaffected by the war that ravaged the land and its people. Open rice patties dotted the south, and to the west and north loomed the stately, yet treacherous mountains of Vietnam. Had it not been for the war, Vietnam would have been a pretty country, although the heat and humidity were oppressive and unrelenting. In spite of the beautiful terrain, I could not imagine living in a steam cooker.

About six o'clock that evening, I heard the angry sounds of gunfire erupting in the distance. My immediate reaction was to duck into a bunker. I had not yet been issued a weapon. The machine gun fire stopped, and artillery batteries commenced firing, still distant, but just as fierce. It was my first taste, sound, and smell of war. The never-ending noise from artillery shells in the distance greeted us in the morning and was the last thing we heard before succumbing to a restless sleep at night. The rat-a-tat-tat of machine gun fire pierced the air again, joining in a dissonant chorus of endless noise. I remember hearing commands I'd never heard before, like "Just get the bombs on the airplanes—I don't care what it takes." Stateside, those same commands had been orderly, but in Vietnam, they carried a frenetic tone. I could see the jet aircraft taking off from Da Nang Air Base; the acrid taste and smell of burning jet fuel stung my nostrils and filled my throat.

Over the next thirteen months, those tastes, sounds, and smells would worsen. But for now, it was exhilarating, and I was ready to fight for a noble cause.

I learned early on not to get close to anyone, mostly because people came and went frequently, due to transfers, changes in orders, and of course, death. I had so many commanding officers, as well as troops with whom I served, I do not recall many of their names, as the constant change and the passage of time have blurred my memory.

The next morning, I reported to the administration office, or S-1, for my assignment. Every Marine pilot's fear was to be sent with ground troops as a Forward Air Controller (FAC), rather than being allowed to fly airplanes, which was what we had trained to do. But it didn't matter to me whether I went with the ground troops or a squadron. I was still enthralled with the excitement of going to war. My mantra repeated in my mind: Victory is our only option. Victory is our only option.

The lieutenant colonel in charge of the S-1 called me in and said, "I'm assigning you to a squadron up near the DMZ at Quang Tri." The squadron, called VMO-6, was a composite squadron containing UH-1Es and the OV-10. The UH-1Es were gunships and used to extract, insert, and protect ground troops. The OV-10 was an observation airplane which was used to locate the enemy and deliver ordnance. I was delighted to be only a lieutenant and assigned directly to a squadron. I caught the helicopter late that afternoon and flew north from Da Nang to Quang Tri.

I arrived without incident, one of two lieutenants and several enlisted Marines assigned to that unit. The sergeant major took the enlisted Marines and pointed me toward the commanding officer's office, a small building shaped like the letter *C*, what many people in the States refer to as a chicken coop.

The CO welcomed me aboard and handed me a check-in sheet mapping out the various places to draw my equipment. He told me to be quick because he was short of pilots and needed me to be flying as soon as possible. I picked up assorted survival equipment, including a radio. Most surprising was the issuance of a chest protector, which was almost an inch thick and weighed around twenty pounds. I asked what it was, although I thought I already knew and was told it was a bullet bouncer. I went to the armory, was issued a .38 pistol, and told I could have all the ammunition I needed, but to start with two boxes. I now had my flight equipment and was ready to go to war. The next day, I flew my first combat mission.

The helicopter gunship lifted off from Quang Tri base at six o'clock in the morning. I was flying with a seasoned combat pilot, a major. There were two enlisted Marines with me, the crew chief, and a gunner. The helicopter was armed with forward firing ordnance that included four machine guns and 2.75-inch rockets. Both the crew chief and the gunner had door-mounted machine guns, which swiveled to various angles so they could also fire out the side. Each person had a pistol, and there was a forty millimeter grenade launcher on board as well. The helicopter was loaded with a tremendous amount of ammunition, C-rations, which were our food, a canteen of water for each person, and a first-aid kit.

My job was to read the map. Unfortunately, for the first four hours of the day, I was totally lost. The major, Ed, was tolerant, having been in my shoes once himself. He would smile and ask me where we were. He would occasionally ask me how to pronounce the name of the place where we were, which I could not do properly. He also let me fly so he could smoke a cigarette, something that would never be allowed in today's aviation. Four months after I transferred out of Quang Tri, I learned that Ed was killed. He served his country honorably and I appreciated the training he gave me. It helped keep me alive.

An hour and a half into the flight we encountered our first enemy engagement. I'll never forget the sound of machine guns and rockets as they were fired directly at enemy positions. I don't know whether we hit any of them, but clouds of dust and debris came up everywhere. I could see them returning fire at us with their tracers. We continued until we had to return to re-arm and refuel at a nearby outpost. I watched as we controlled our first air strike that day with the major calculating where the aircraft would drop their bombs and napalm. I was amazed at the skill with which he maneuvered our UH-1E into position to allow the jets to drop their ordnance close to the ground troops, always ensuring it dropped on the enemy, and not our troops. His masterful coordination of this effort was a work of art. His precision and firm resolve to give only his best set a good example for me. The major's advice resonated with me. "No matter how hard it gets, never let it be said you dropped ordnance on friendly troops." I memorized his counsel and vowed adherence to it.

We kept the helicopter all day, returning it at six o'clock in the evening—a twelve-hour day. We'd been shot at, but fortunately, not hit. This wouldn't be the case in the thirteen months that followed, but I returned safely after my introduction to combat flying in Vietnam. After that first day, reality hit me hard. This was not a game—it was for real. I could be shot or killed. I realized fear that first night as I lay in bed—fear of letting my fellow Marines down—and fear of not going home. Those fears were real to me, and I spent time in prayer asking God for courage. While I was grateful that my first time out I emerged intact, there would be well over six hundred combat missions for me, some from which I would not emerge unscathed.

It wasn't long before I began to compute time in months, rather than days and weeks. The days became the same, each day an indistinguishable blur from the one before it or after it. Every day was a combat day, every night a combat mission, and they ran together, each spilling over into the next. Time ceased to exist. I soon lost track of what day it was, unable to discern Sunday from Monday or Tuesday. I was only able to go to chapel for memorial services if I wasn't flying, however, I flew every day. I carried a New Testament with me in my flight suit pocket and had my quiet time early every morning with the Lord. I don't know how the men without a personal relationship with God made it through the war.

Each day, we were assigned a mission. It might be to escort a convoy, do a medivac extraction, assist troops in contact, or be coordinated with part of a huge assault. Time, whenever I was able to grasp its concept, was measured only by how many months I had left to serve.

During the rare moments I was not flying, my time was spent writing home and sleeping. I was always bone-tired at the end of the day. The food wasn't bad, but we burned a lot of calories, and almost everyone was skinny. The routine was always the same: pick up your airplane, fly all day, shoot and be shot at, return, and take a shower. The shower was nothing more than rainwater caught in fifty-five-gallon barrels placed on a wooden stand. I ate whatever food I could, and slept.

The housing was referred to as the Southeast Asia Sea Hut. Each hooch housed eight of us. Our beds were always damp. I never knew if it was from the humidity or the rain. Every night I laid down on a wet bed with my head on a wet pillow before getting up to repeat it all over again in the sweltering heat. We made these sacrifices to keep our beloved nation free.

We built bunkers near the housing because we were frequently rocketed, and snipers would fire from across the river. When this evolution started, we would grab our weapons and race toward the bunker. A rocket landing on our hooch could cost us our lives, but we were safe in a bunker. Occasionally, a snake or rat would crawl in there; that's why I always stopped to put on my boots before entering. The bunkers were made of iron beams, sandbags, and concrete. They were similar to the bunkers in other wars, and we would head for the shelter they provided each time the rocket attacks started.

Quite a lot of drinking went on. For some, it was the only way they could cope with the stress of war.

One evening, as dusk was settling in, one of the majors—not the one I first flew with, got drunk, really drunk, falling down, stupid drunk. The shelling began and, like always, we started to run toward the bunkers. But the major was so drunk, he'd passed out. My buddy, Lieutenant Lenart and I couldn't leave him on the ground—he'd be killed for sure, so we each took an arm and pulled him toward safety. The incapacitated major was dead weight, and as we dragged him, his face was only inches from the sand, and his feet were trailing behind him, leaving grooves in the sand. At the precise moment we reached the bunker, the major woke up and lifted his head, banging it hard on the railroad tie that acted as a support beam. This, of course, resulted in a knockout, and an enormous goose egg formed on his head, as the major dropped back to the ground.

I said to Lenart, "We gotta get him into the bunker."

Lenart refused and said, "I'm not goin' out there and get shot for him."

So we dragged the major in by his feet.

In the morning, the major did not remember anything from the previous evening. All he could say was, "How'd I get this bump on my head?" No one said a word. Everyone had been busy scrambling into the bunkers, and of course, neither Lenart nor I had any desire to tell the major he had us to thank for saving his sorry self, and maybe he should rethink his choice of beverage. So we never told him. Some things are best left unsaid.

But even in the midst of war, danger, and tragedy, we still managed to find a little comic relief.

In an effort, I suppose, to boost morale, the military, on occasion, provided entertainment for the troops. The entertainment the military provided was lacking in, well, everything. Night after night, it was the same old John Wayne movie. We had an old reel projector, and each evening the entertainment was provided, it was *Hondo and the Indian*. Every. Single. Night. We reached a point where we had all memorized the *entire* movie, including every word of the dialogue. For fun, we'd start the reel, turn off the sound, and we would say the words of each character as we watched the show. I played John Wayne. One of our guys had some Indian heritage, so he always played Hondo. We even called him Chief. Everyone would say their lines as the soundless movie played. So we provided our own entertainment, with *Hondo and the Indian* as the background. It was infinitely more fun than watching the same movie over and over and over.

One night, we *finally* had some live entertainment, for a welcome change. A Filipino band performed for us. There are no words that can describe what it was like listening to American songs sung with a heavy Filipino accent. To say something was lacking, doesn't even come close. At least it wasn't *Hondo and the Indian*, and was, in any event, entertaining. One of the female singers sang *Ring of Fire*, by Johnny Cash. When she got to the words "burn, burn, burn," she whisked off her top. The guys all went nuts, and one of the pilots, who stood six foot four inches, got so excited, he jumped up with his hands reaching straight into the air—right into the overhead metal fan. He cut his hands badly and was rushed to treatment. His executive officer was so mad he gave the poor guy only three days off to heal, before sending him out to fly again.

While our entertainment was nothing to write home about, I did appreciate that at least an effort had been made. It helped kill time. The best entertainment I had was when I got to fly gun cover for Bob Hope, although from high up in my helicopter I didn't get to see him.

Near the DMZ, I became familiar with places like Hue, Khe Sanh, and others, names now etched in our nation's history. The countryside was mountainous and would have been beautiful, had it not been for the craters left by constant bombing and shelling. The standing joke told to the new guys was that they couldn't go home until they had filled in all the bomb holes. I wouldn't be surprised if those bomb craters are still there.

There was no such thing as a routine mission. The term milk run was never applied to anything I ever flew, whether it was gun cover for a truck convoy or engaging the enemy in a fire fight. Every day was unique, bringing new challenges and dangers, and leaving the imprint of particular missions forever engraved in my mind.

I believe it is imperative to memorialize some of my war stories, however, not for purposes of glory or glamorizing war. War is neither glorious nor glamorous. It is important because we, the young soldiers, sailors, airmen, and Marines, answered our nation's call, even though much of the nation never supported us. Not while we were over there, nor when we came home, often broken and irreparably damaged, physically, emotionally, mentally, and spiritually. We were forgotten; cast aside, because our war was a black mark in America's history. But history needs to be accurately learned, and if the truth is ugly, then it's ugly. Truth is truth, regardless of how anybody feels about it. It's important to know what happened, not from a historian or politician, but from someone who was there. That is why I will share a few of my many stories.

One such story begins on a day while standing on alert, we were mobilized to help extract a Marine reconnaissance team which had captured an enemy soldier. Their prisoner was an enemy advisor from a country other than North Vietnam. The Marines were outnumbered, ten to one. It was our mission to go in and get this Marine recon team and the enemy they had captured before they were killed or captured.

Our extraction group was made up of four helicopters: two UH-1Es, and two H-46s. The H-46s were the helicopters the troops would climb aboard while we provided fire cover. As we approached the landing zone where we were to extract the Marines and their prisoner, the lead aircraft, the UH-1E, called to the Marines on the ground and asked if the zone was secure. In a low whispering voice, the Marine on the ground said, "Yes, sir, the zone is secure."

The lead helicopter responded, "Why are you whispering?"

The response, again in a low, whispering voice, reported that his side of the landing zone was secure. The helicopter pilot asked, "If only your side is secure, how large is the landing zone?"

The whispering voice responded, "Thirty meters."

A long silence followed, and then the lead helicopter gunship said to us, "Let's go get them."

While we were in that zone covering the troop helicopters, the exchange of firepower from both sides was enormous and deafening. This was the first battle I had fought where a bullet struck *my* helicopter. The fighting was fierce and the noise unending. The odds were against us, as the shelling rained bullets around us like a hailstorm, but the mission was critical. It was a difficult challenge, but we prevailed and got those Marines and their prisoner out. The enemy continued shooting in a furious and relentless attempt to bring us down, even after we were long out of range. The team leader radioed ahead that we had the recon team with some wounded, *and* their live prisoner.

When we returned to base, the wounded were taken for medical treatment, and we were met by a large contingent of armed security. I was not allowed into the debriefing room where the prisoner was held, but I was told that the prisoner's nationality was Chinese. I never knew for certain, but we obviously had a prisoner who was considered valuable concerning information he had of our enemy. Our mission was a success but involved the most intense and prolonged combat since my arrival in Vietnam.

On another occasion, I was flying with a different major, whose name I can't recall, at about fifteen hundred feet. He looked out of his window and said, "I think I saw some bushes move."

I glanced over at him and thought, Yeah, right. You're at fifteen hundred feet, and you saw a bush move.

Without another word, he rolled the helicopter to a nearly inverted position and started shooting at a bunch of bushes in an open field, at which point, about thirty of these bushes started to run full blast across the field. Every bush was carrying a rifle. That was the good news. The bad news was that the helicopter went into a blade stall, which is caused when the tips of the rotor blade start to go supersonic, that is, faster than the speed of sound. This rendered the helicopter almost uncontrollable until he got the speed down. The blade stall was caused by the violent maneuver the major had performed to put the helicopter into position to shoot these bushes. As we plummeted out of control toward earth, we were no longer interested in the bushes running across the field. We were too busy trying to regain control of our helicopter. We did so, but not until we came dangerously close to hitting the ground. I don't remember the exact footage, but the trees and bushes we were chasing were extremely close. I also remember that they had been running and stopped and stared at the helicopter. They just stared, didn't even bother to shoot at us. I imagined they were thinking this is going to be some air show, followed by a crash. When we recovered the helicopter and were flying home, they didn't shoot at us, and we didn't shoot at them anymore.

The major never said a word. After we landed back at home base and were walking away from the helicopter, he turned to me and said, "I hope you learned something today."

I smiled at him and answered, "Yes, sir. I sure did." I learned he was a pompous lunatic, and I hoped I would never have to fly with him again.

I flew approximately two months with VMO-6 near the DMZ, when I received orders to join a new squadron, VMO-2. The V stands for fixed wing; the M stands for Marine; and the O stands for observation. This squadron was located at Marble Mountain, on the shore of the South China Sea. Approximately two miles west of us was the Da Nang airbase. VMO-2 had UH-1Es, AH1-Gs, which we picked up in April 1969, and the OV-10A. I had the privilege of flying all three of these aircraft while serving in that squadron.

This transfer took place in April 1969. Most of my combat flying was with VMO-2. Places like Elephant Valley, Monkey Mountain, Hill 55, and An Hoa, were now familiar, along with many nameless places to the far West. For the entire month of January, I flew the UH-1E and the OV-10. I grew up quickly that January and received my designation as a section lead, which included two airplanes, and a division lead, which included four airplanes. I was responsible for those aircraft and the men that flew them—a somber responsibility that I took seriously. Every day we flew, someone would execute an extraordinary event that to us was considered ordinary. We were just doing our jobs.

During this time, the stark reality which the effects of war ravaged on the human psyche began to manifest itself with somber clarity. Some dealt with the stress and strain by drinking too much. Others experienced mood swings. Two had complete emotional breakdowns and were sent home. War changes everybody, as body and mind struggle to deal with extreme stress in extreme conditions, above and beyond that which we were created to handle. The results can be lifelong and heartbreaking. The glory and glamour of war had faded to black as the grief of ruined lives lay heavily on me. This could not have been God's plan for humankind.

Each of us dealt with the stress of war differently. It was my goal to remain focused on the task at hand, believing God would deal with me as He saw fit. I was going to try to fly every day, write a letter home, and sleep a lot. Several of the other pilots overwhelmed with stress, either could not or would not fly at some point, so I took their flights. By taking their flights in addition to mine, I amassed a total of over twelve hundred flight hours on a combination of four different aircraft, helicopter and fixed wing, the most of any combat pilot in my squadron. Flying was *my* way of dealing with the stress. I was relieved when I got back, and my enemy didn't.

If I wasn't flying, I was sleeping. Instead of writing to Arleen every day, I was only writing once a week, partly because by this time, there was simply nothing new to say. What could I write? I had eggs again today for breakfast? I bombed all day today? Again. And again. Also, I didn't want to tell Arleen the truth as to what was really happening on the other side of the world.

I missed Arleen more than anything. Knowing she was waiting for my return and keeping our home going gave me the strength and will to go one more day.

The miles between us did nothing to dim our love and longing to be together.

Arleen and I invented ways to communicate with each other beyond the exchange of letters. Our first inspiration was to record our conversations on tape. That didn't work out very well, because we never got the tape recorder speeds correct, and invariably, the reels of tape would either be crushed or otherwise destroyed by the time I received them in the mail. Undaunted, we became more creative and reached each other through ham radio operators. In the middle of the night, I would go to the communications center and try to call home. The transmissions were often faded or broken. It was mandatory to end each sentence with the word over. Therefore, our conversations went something like:

"I am fine, over."

"It is raining here, over."

"I love you, over."

Half the time, all we ever heard was *over*. It was frustrating and comical at the same time, but I look back at the memories and am warmed by the commitment of our young love, and our determination to keep it strong. Each trial and hardship we went through served as another building block in our marriage.

Eventually, we returned to writing. Writing helped me escape the pressure of combat. My faith in God and the comfort of knowing He was always with me, helped me face the strain of my battle. Knowing that at any moment I could breathe my last breath, brought me closer to God than I had ever been.

Three times I've heard the last words of dying men: "God save me, I am dying."

On military aircraft, whether helicopter or fixed wing, the button you push to talk on the radio is located on either the flight control stick or the engine throttle. Many times, in desperate or tense situations, a pilot will squeeze the stick and throttle very hard, inadvertently keying the radio transmission button.

The first time I heard these words was when a troop transport helicopter was hovering above the tree level with a hoist down through the trees, extracting a wounded Marine. There had been no exchange of hostile gunfire, and we were circling overhead, ensuring he had safe cover. Suddenly, either by enemy fire, mechanical failure, or pilot error, the helicopter pitched violently onto its side, crashing into the trees and bursting into flames. Just as the helicopter began to roll on its side, one of the pilots, clinging tightly to the flight controls, screamed his last words, "God save us, we're dying!" It took us the rest of the afternoon to recover the dead from the helicopter. I hoped this brave pilot had turned to God before that tragic day. The somber moment when you hear these words weighs heavy on your heart. You *never* forget it.

Two months later, a UH-1E rolled in on an enemy position when it was hit by enemy ground fire and burst into flames. As it crashed to the ground, one of the pilots pushed the radio button and shouted, "God help us, we're dying!"

Two and a half months after that incident, a fixed-wing aircraft was shot down. The pilot screamed the same words, just before hitting the ground, "God save me, I'm dying!"

These three events had a marked effect on my life. I can never forget hearing the same last words screamed from the lips of dying men, crying for help from the only possible source of hope; God. Men and women of war stay close to Him, for He is your only hope of salvation.

February ushered in the monsoon season. It was 1969. I had never seen rain like that in my entire life!

It rained all day, nearly every day, and it was always cloudy. When the monsoons came, the level of fighting dropped off significantly. Our forces, the North Vietnamese, and the Viet Cong were hampered by the weather. I suppose our enemy was just as miserable as we were. With the rains came the floods and we spent much of our time rescuing Marines and others trapped in flood waters. I flew some, but most of my missions were either re-supply or pulling a soldier or sailor out of the flood waters. Flying in bad weather, occasionally contact was made with enemy troops, and those skirmishes would result in our troops requiring medivac.

We lived in tin huts built like chicken coops. Everything was always damp, and nothing ever completely dried. Arleen sent me an electric blanket because we sometimes had generators. When I was gone during the day flying, I would turn on the electric blanket, and it would sometimes dry out the bed. Dampness was everywhere, and we were continually wet, getting into the airplanes to fly. The weather was so bad sometimes, it limited the flying, but it never stopped us completely.

Then came the Tet Offensive of 1969. Tet is the Vietnamese New Year celebration. Because this is a special time of year in Vietnam, our enemy strategized that we would assume they would not attack, and we would be relaxed. In 1968, we were caught off-guard, but in 1969, we were better prepared. It would be an understatement to say that all hell broke loose. I don't know whether the Tet of 1968 or 1969 was worse. Whichever Tet Offensive you were in was the worst. Fighting erupted all over South Vietnam. In response, we dropped bombs on North Vietnam. It was a violent time—one I hope to never see again.

I left VMO-2 for six weeks to fly the TA4 Skyhawk, a jet, denoting targets in North and South Vietnam.

I liked flying the TA4 Skyhawk, marking targets for the bombers that flew off the ships in the South China Sea, and near the DMZ. Once near the DMZ, I ran into heavy anti-aircraft FLAK, but by the third time they shot at me, I recognized what it was, and began evasive maneuvers. I would continue on my mission, always hoping to see the burst of the shell being fired first. I had been told it was the one you didn't see that got you, so I was diligently on the lookout. God's hand was on me, but I never took the Lord's protection for granted. I sometimes returned with a few holes in my airplane, but I always came back. Many did not.

We were in the middle of a surge operation at this time. In a surge operation, you continually reload, re-arm, and take off as fast as you can because the battle-field is very intense. It is chaotic and nerve-wracking, as everyone is working as hard and as quickly as they can. There are no slow-downs or breaks. It's difficult to be calm at such a frenetic pace.

Once, when I was flying the TA4 during a surge operation, I saw, in the midst of this chaos, a man who was remarkably composed. This Marine was the calmest, coolest, most collected individual I had ever seen. Surge operations were in full swing, and as fast as we could reload and re-arm the airplane, we would take off to again drop on our assigned targets.

There was a load of bombs on the back of a trail-er being pulled to reload airplanes. As the ordnance crew was going down the middle of the flight ramp, one of these bombs rolled off the trailer, down the flight line, and was rolling toward this Marine. A five-hundred-pound bomb will destroy a large house. The Marine stood where he was and simply watched his impending death barreling toward him until it rolled to a stop about twenty feet from him. To my surprise, the bomb did not detonate, but this Marine calmly stopped, looked around, and stuck both fingers in his

ears, as if to say the only thing I can save is my hearing because the rest of me will be blown to pieces.
He didn't panic. He was simply calm and matter-of-fact
about a situation that we all expected would blow him
to smithereens. I would often think of him, and regret
not having an opportunity to talk to him about this incident. I should have gone back and met him, but in
the heat of battle, we just kept going.

Toward the middle of March 1969, my commanding officer chose five from our squadron to go to Vũng
Tàu, southeast of Saigon, to learn to fly the Cobra
Helicopter Gunship, AH-1G. The Army already had
them, and the Marine Corps were getting them. I was
among the five assigned to Vũng Tàu to learn to fly
the Cobra with the United States Army. Although I'd
long lost my enthusiasm for war, I never lost my love
of flying, whether it was in a helicopter or fixed-wing
aircraft. The sky was my limit, and I looked forward to
seeing what capabilities the Cobra possessed.

I was impressed with the training we received in
the classroom. The Army knew the systems, the helicopter, and how to fly it. In the ground school, we
learned how the weapons system worked. The Cobra
gunships carried two people—the co-pilot in the front
and the pilot in the back. The cockpit was approximately one hundred inches wide. The nose turret in
this model shot a forty millimeter grenade launcher
from one side, and on the other, the machine gun shot
7.62-millimeter rounds. The pilot in the back fired
the wing-mounted stations, i.e., rockets, or machine
guns, and they were strictly gunship in support of the
ground troops. In Vũng Tàu, our days consisted of
a morning ground school where we learned the aircraft's systems, and in the afternoon, we would fly.

Vũng Tàu was an interesting city because it was
believed that the Viet Cong used it as their place for
rest and relaxation, R&R for short. We were told that

if we went out into the village, which I only did on one occasion, we should take our pistol and wear it under our shirt. They did not want anyone to be seen with weapons. The village was unique in that respect.

During our training missions, we would practice flying the aircraft with takeoffs and landings. Then, we learned how to deliver ordnance. Some of these training missions were actual combat missions we flew with their aircraft. Sometimes we would be called to leave the security of our airbase, where we were practicing our landing, and go out and shoot the rockets and machine guns.

In Vũng Tàu, we stayed in what had at one time been the home of a French doctor. It was a villa that had been converted into classrooms and living quarters, and it was quite nice.

The rain had finally gone, and the weather returned to its familiar sticky, humid, heat. I ventured into the village with a friend, neither of us openly carrying our weapon. When we would pass someone on the street that was not South Vietnamese, the looks they gave us led us to believe they were either regular NVA or Viet Cong on R&R. The town never took any rockets, and neither did the airbase, because of the rumor that it was a place at which the enemy took their R&R. Although this was never confirmed, I had no problem believing it.

At the completion of that three and a half-weeks training, the five of us returned to our base, Marble Mountain, near the seashore, and received our Cobras in April 1969. There were four brand new Cobras for the five of us, presented at a ceremony at the airbase where the Army turned them over. We started flying them the next day. My squadron used three different types of aircraft now; the Cobras, the UH-1E, and the OV-10 Bronco. I was privileged to fly all of them on their assigned missions. The Cobra helicopter was the one in which I engaged the enemy most often in South Vietnam. I was involved in many, many firefights.

You can never know courage until you have known fear. I was flying the UH-1E gunship when I was shot down in May 1969. We had lifted out of An Hoa. Four of us were on board: Major Mason was the pilot, I, still, a lieutenant was the co-pilot. We had a gunner, Tom, and a crew chief, Mike, with us. We had just lifted up after rearming and refueling and were between fifteen hundred and eighteen hundred feet when ground fire hit our helicopter, and it burst into flames. We always flew in pairs, so Mel, our wingman in the second helicopter, saw what had happened. Following normal procedure, he took over to coordinate the rescue effort, so those in the emergency aircraft only had to worry about getting it to the ground. Night was beginning to fall, exacerbating our situation.

When a fixed-wing airplane bursts into flames, you should eject. However, you *never* eject from a helicopter. It would be like a banana going through a fan. You must ride it down and complete autorotation.

We were going down, but the wind coming through the roller blades provided energy to turn them, and that prevented us from a free-fall. As we were heading down, I looked at what I thought appeared to be a road, but it was difficult to tell because it was dusk. The impending darkness masked the landing zone. It looked like a road, so we headed for it.

Instead of shouting, "Mayday, mayday," Mel, a country boy, in his good ole Southern Tennessee drawl, calmly announced, "Jackson, that thing is really burning. I don't think you're gonna make it."

Not in the mood for friendly chit-chat, I answered, "Just get on the ground and pick me up." I was angry at the situation because I'd lost this battle. I was not afraid to die, but I believed this was not my time. As we were auto-rotating down, we discovered that what we thought in the darkness was a road, was, in fact, a huge gulley. In other words, this was not going to be a textbook landing. The helicopter hit on the side of the gulley and pitched up on its nose. We landed with the tail of the aircraft straight up, and the nose straight down. It rocked back and forth momentarily, and I thought it was going to go over. Gasoline and fire pouring around us, I felt for a moment that Arleen would soon be a widow. But the Lord had other ideas. The helicopter rocked back, hit on its skids and settled into the ditch.

We all scrambled out of the aircraft—or so I thought. We headed down the gulley as fast as we could go. Two people ran in front of me, but in the midst of our mad dash to escape the enemy, I felt the Lord prompting me to look back to see where our fourth person was. I'm thankful I heeded the prompting because when I turned around, I saw Tom, our gunner, trapped in the helicopter. The enemy was still relentlessly shooting at us, but fortunately, I was down in the gulley. Racing back as fast as I could, amid a shower of enemy fire, I pulled the gunner out of the aircraft, loosening his belts, cords, and ammo. Two enemies came up on the edge of the ditch. I fired at them, and Tom and I raced to the rescue helicopter.

By the grace of God, all four of us got out and lived to tell about it. Had I not returned for Tom, he would have been killed. Later, he thanked me for coming back for him. Had any of us failed to escape, we would not have been captured—we would have been killed. As we pulled away, we could see some of the enemy coming near the helicopter. At this time, our other wingman arrived and began to deliver ordnance, forcing the enemy to retreat from the smoldering helicopter.

Months passed before I returned to flying OV-10s and marking targets with white phosphorous rounds. I flew every day, all day. My goal was to while away the hours in the cockpit engaged in combat. I didn't want to stay out of duty, and I did not want to be in my hooch unless I was sleeping. So, I flew and fought, flew and fought, day after day, unable to distinguish any day of the week from another. I only knew which day was Sunday because we were issued our malaria pills on Sundays. Those pills made me so sick I finally decided after seven months, that it would be easier to get malaria, so without telling anyone else, I quit taking the pills. I felt much better, and never ended up getting the disease anyway.

War is rife with tragedy, exacting a heavy toll on everybody and everything it touches. The ravages of war leave no one unscathed, even if they return whole in body. Loss, while inevitable, is still a devastating heartbreak. Lives full of promise are cut short decades early, leaving a trail of grief and sorrow as to what could have been. Those who remain may suffer from survivor's guilt, as they try to deal with unfathomable loss and struggle to understand why they lived and their friend did not. We live in a fallen and broken world, however, war is not the cause of the brokenness. It is the result.

Ken Pennington was a good friend of mine in my squadron who arrived in Vietnam a week ahead of me. He flew the gunship escort for the medivacs. During the heavy rains of the monsoons, we received a call to pick up some wounded Marines. Unfortunately, Ken launched by himself. As he searched above the clouds to where he thought was the location of the injured Marines, he began to let his helicopter down to pick them up. He headed toward the light coming out of the clouds. But he'd gotten the wrong location, and had let down over an enemy base camp. They immediately started firing at Ken and hit his helicopter. He managed to get back up into the clouds, but he crashed with little information radioed to home base as to his location.

In the wee hours of the morning, we received word that Ken was missing. Because Ken and I were close friends, this news struck me hard. I picked up the medivac, and we immediately launched. We searched the rest of the night, into the morning, and the rest of the following day. I flew long hours and came back tired, to get another airplane. We would engage the enemy when we found them, but finding Ken was our number one goal.

On the evening of the second day, we found Lieutenant Ken Pennington lying against a wall in an open meadow, wounded and severely burned. I picked him up and brought him to the hospital. Later that evening, I visited him. He was barely recognizable because of his terrible injuries, but he still had the heart and soul of a very dear friend. He passed away the next morning from his injuries. Even through the pain of his burns and wounds, Ken Pennington set a courageous example for all to appreciate and respect. He had taken off at night in terrible weather to find and rescue injured Marines. He could have waited until it was safer to leave, but his hero heart would not allow him that luxury while brothers-in-arms lay wounded and waiting. Every man and woman who makes the ultimate sacrifice for their country should hold a place of honor in the hearts of Americans.

My commanding officer assigned me the difficult task of going through Ken's personal effects, packing them up, and mailing them to his family. Unfortunately, I never saw his family because I was still in Vietnam when Ken was honorably laid to rest. I lost track of the Pennington family, but never his memory.

Other friends were also lost, and their memorial services held. Life goes on, but in a diminished capacity, leaving more questions than answers, and the unending grappling of those left behind, of what would have been had there not been a war at all.

It doesn't matter which war was fought. I imagine there were mothers and fathers who asked George Washington why their sons and daughters died. Loved ones asked this of former presidents, Jefferson, Lincoln, Roosevelt, Truman, Reagan, Clinton, Bush, Obama, and now, our current president, Trump. Every parent, spouse, and child of a fallen warrior asks why their loved one died. My answer is both simple and complex. Within the soul of every human being is a longing for freedom. God placed this desire within us. The problem, however, in our fallen state, is that freedom is not free. It comes at a very dear price. Throughout the history of our country, warriors have fallen to preserve the freedoms of which many citizens of the United States of America tend to take advantage. I was privileged and humbled to have served with some of those heroes. Unless and until man learns to respect the freedom of everyone, there will always be war.

As July 1969 approached, I'd been in Vietnam nearly eight months. I'd earned some R&R, and my lovely wife and I devised a wonderful and much-needed plan to spend five days and four nights in Hong Kong. I hadn't seen Arleen since I left the previous October. I missed her terribly and longed to be with her. I waited until I was well over half-way through my tour to take my R&R, and wanted at least most of the war behind me before I saw Arleen again.

I headed for Hong Kong where we'd picked the hotel. I couldn't get there fast enough.

Arleen arrived in Hong Kong the day before I did. I arrived around noon and raced to the hotel to find her. When I asked the clerk what room Mrs. Jackson was in, he gave me the room number, and I ran up to the room and knocked on the door. The door opened wide, and there stood not my beautiful Arleen, but a *man*!

I asked, "Is Mrs. Jackson in this room?"

He replied, "No, Marine, there's no Mrs. Jackson here. Just my wife."

Flustered at what had happened, I raced back downstairs and asked where Mrs. Jackson was. The clerk gave me another room number. Hurrying to the new room, I again knocked on the door, and another man answered. Once again, I asked if Mrs. Jackson was there. She was, but it was not *my* Mrs. Jackson.

I began to worry. Had Arleen missed her connection? Was she stranded somewhere, alone in a strange country? Once again, I returned to the front desk. This time, I learned that Arleen did not like our first room, so she requested a different one. I went to yet a third room and knocked on that door. The third time was definitely a charm—there stood my beautiful Arleen!

We enjoyed five fabulous days. We toured Hong Kong and ate in nice restaurants. We took rickshaw rides and purchased souvenirs we still have. We walked on the piers, marveling at the people who lived in the sand pans, the little boats, and how they lived on the hillside.

After five glorious days, I bid Arleen farewell and told her I'd be home for Christmas. My heart ached as she boarded her plane, and once again the separation of war weighed on my soul. Later that same day, I flew back to Da Nang.

CHAPTER 8
Battle Fatigue

During August, September, and October of 1969, the war turned up several notches. Everywhere I went, I was engaged in supporting troops and pulling out medivacs. I had just landed after a two and a half-hour mission in the OV-10, in one-hundred-degree weather, and walked into the operations briefing area.

The duty officer greeted me with, "Jack, there're troops in contact. We need your watch right away."

I immediately turned around, oblivious to the heat and the fatigue, and rushed to the airplane assigned to me. It was time once again, to kill the enemy, and to race toward victory. Suddenly, I stopped. To my horror, I realized that I was beginning to *enjoy* the fighting and the killing. It had become an adrenaline rush, and I was troubled to realize that I could even think in such a way. I'd lost my focus as to why I was there. I had gone with the sole purpose of serving my country, but in the midst of doing so, I lost that purpose in the noise and turmoil of battle, and everything had become a game—a game which I was horrified to admit I now enjoyed. Nothing else mattered. I was unsure if I would be able to refocus if the war ended. Could I adjust to normal family life as a mere civilian? *What was happening to me?*

I completed the mission and returned safely to base. My commanding officer wanted to talk with me, so I headed for his office. I didn't share my thoughts with him. I wanted them buried deep inside me where they could never surface. I'd become immune to the reason we were even in Vietnam in the first place. I craved the adrenaline rush and success that came with winning a battle, neither comprehending nor caring that it was I who had caused an enemy to lose his life. This enemy was somebody's husband, father, son, or brother. It mattered not that I brought untold grief to a family to the same degree the families of my fallen comrades suffered. While this now matters a great deal to me, at that time, the excitement of victory was all I could taste. I knew it was wrong.

I still had my quiet time early every morning with the Lord. But when it was time to go to work, I closed my Bible and went to work. Quiet time was quiet time. Work was work. I was now adept at compartmentalizing the few facets into which my life had been condensed. No compartment bled over into the next.

My commanding officer offered a seat across from him, and I sat, waiting to learn what my next mission was. But I was disappointed to learn I had not been summoned to receive another mission.

He was quiet for a few moments, and I was getting antsy for more work. When he spoke, his words were deliberate and thoughtful. "Jack, you look tired."

"I'm fine, sir."

"You've flown thirty-three percent more missions than any other pilot. That would make most pilots pretty tired."

"Not me, sir. I'm ready to go!"

"Jack, does December 30 mean anything to you?"

I gave the date some thought, but couldn't think of anything specific. I shook my head.

"No? What about April 5? Ring any bells?"

I had no idea what my CO was getting at. Each day was like all the others—they ran together, and nothing stood out as being more notable than any other. Why was he throwing random dates at me? I was good at winning the game. It was time to go fly again.

"Does August 12 carry any significance for you?"

I thought, but nothing came to mind. There were no days that were special or stood out for any reason that I could recall. I wished he would stop and let me get back to the game. Again, I shook my head.

"Jack, December 30 is your wedding anniversary. April 5 is Arleen's birthday, and Jacky was born on August 12."

I was stunned. I had forgotten three of the most important dates in my life. *How could I have forgotten?* Far from home and family, far from the happy, clean comforts of the only life I'd known, having my brain rattled with the incessant cacophony of artillery fire, bombs, the cries of the injured and of the dying, and every other horror of war—somewhere in the web of survival in a surreal environment, my mind was altered, as it bore the ravages of this great conflict. In the intense stress of always being "on" every waking moment, knowing my situation mandated that I had to kill or be killed, the glory of war quickly fades, as the lines of sanity and insanity and the clear demarcation of right and wrong begin to blur, and a new reality emerges. The human psyche was not designed to endure such prolonged and intense stress, and I was now claimed as its most recent victim.

My commanding officer had enough experience to recognize battle fatigue when he saw it. Today we call it post-traumatic stress disorder, and I was a textbook case. He wanted me to take some R&R. I needed a few days off to go someplace and relax. He sent me to a jungle training school in the Philippines at the Subic Bay Naval Base. I flew there, got a room at the Officer's Club, and checked into the survival school. They trained me during the day, but the afternoons and evenings were free. I spent time by the pool, relaxing and eating good meals.

Away from the stress of war, the incessant noise, the death and loss, and alone with my thoughts, my sanity eventually returned, and my focus became clear again. Rest is critical if healing from PTSD is to occur. The mind and body are on overload, resulting in physiological changes that, if not addressed and treated properly, can become permanent.

While my mind was altered in the surreal setting of war, I never rejected my faith, but it wasn't as clear as when I was home in a peaceful setting where a church was found on every corner. I was aware of God, but in a different mind-set—one of unclear thinking. We were all so young, and although we had been well-trained for battle, we were not prepared emotionally for what lay ahead. I went from guns, guts, and glory to being broken. I may not have understood what was happening to me, but God did, and He never left me through this difficult time. It was only by the grace of God that I got through this. Only God can bring the peace that passes all understanding, regardless of the turmoil that we may find ourselves in the midst of.

In time, I was fortunate to recover enough from the post-traumatic stress that I was able to live a normal life and keep my emotions in check. While nobody fully recovers from PTSD, some recover more than others. War changes a person permanently. Not all veterans do recover, however, and they spend the rest of their lives reliving their battles, over and over, in an unending circle. At night, their dreams are haunted, and by day, they are never free from the chains of the terrors they witnessed and the screams of agony as their friends lay dying. Some suffer from survivor's guilt because their friends did not come home and they did. The burden is too heavy to bear. Some turn to drugs or alcohol; some, unable to ever find peace, commit suicide; marriages fail, and some lives are shattered to the point they can never be whole. War changes everyone, but those who never recover deserve an extra measure of compassion. This war was not a sporting event where there is a winner or loser. Human lives were at stake, and each time a life was lost, a soul was violently hurled into eternity. As a naïve young farm boy, I began my military career by being attracted to the uniforms, but all that changed to a heartfelt desire to serve my country to the best of my ability, and that desire continues to this day. I served because I believed my country wanted me to help stem the tide of Communism in Vietnam. When I returned home, however, I would learn that this was the furthest thing from the truth.

The five days of R&R refreshed me, and I returned to base to spend my last ninety days in this war-torn land. I flew again every day, all day. It wasn't until my last week that they cut back my flying. Three days before I returned home, I flew my final combat mission.

CHAPTER 9

Homecoming

The best feeling in the world was boarding the TWA flight and taking off for *HOME*! The plane was packed full of Marines returning home. We were told not to bring any weapons back for souvenirs. I had a nine millimeter I had used a couple of times. It was a sentimental piece, but I thought better of packing it because the rules were clear that we were not to bring weapons home, and for a change, I felt like obeying the rules.

After the long flight back, we landed at Travis Air Force Base in California. When we arrived, we were asked to empty our sea bags and leave them out for inspection. The gunnery sergeant looked at me and told me to go through without inspecting my sea bag. If I had put that weapon in, I probably would've gotten caught. We were the lucky ones; we had our BPH Medals—our Boarding Pass Home.

I was to meet Arleen in Chicago, the closest airport to where she was staying in Indiana. As I left San Francisco, I changed out of my utilities into my regular Marine uniform, as I had no civilian clothes with me. Taking off from San Francisco felt great! As the airplane took off and began to gain altitude, the TWA pilot, for some reason I'll never understand, pulled the power to idle, causing the plane to drop. Then he pushed it back up to full throttle, and the airplane resumed its climb. I thought to myself that I had been fighting for over a year, facing danger at every turn, and now, I would die off the end of the runway in San Francisco—within the confines of the United States of America, but dead nonetheless. Still today, I have no idea why the pilot did that.

I was excited to see my wife and daughter. What happened next, though, deeply affected me. I was wearing my Marine uniform. Having been at war for so long, I had no idea that we who served were being subjected to hostilities by the people of our own country upon our return. While I was in Vietnam, the only communications I received were letters from home, and one newspaper, the *Stars and Stripes*. The *Stars and Stripes* printed baseball scores and information. We had no access to news reports or any other papers, and we were unaware of and unprepared for the anger and disrespect that would greet us when we finally reached home.

Our plane landed in Chicago. *At last!* I was so happy to be home! As I walked out of the airplane onto the jetway to go into the airport, a man in a business suit pushed me from behind and snarled, "Get out of the way, you sonofabitch."

I was shocked by this disrespectful and uncalled for behavior and was tempted to grab him and rip his lips off. But I didn't want to come off the jetway in handcuffs trying to hug Arleen whom I had only seen for five days in the last thirteen months. I let it go. I wouldn't know this sorry excuse for a man if I saw him today, but that incident profoundly disturbed me. I believed the entire time I served in Vietnam, that I had the support of the American people. I had no reason to believe anything to the contrary. The harsh reality was that I did *not* have their support, and neither did anyone else who served over there.

I was confused. I had no idea how hated we were until I got home. Then I became angry. I never regretted serving my country, and I would do it again without hesitation, but I did feel betrayed by the hypocritical politicians. They had asked us to serve, showering us with flowery speeches and praise, but when we returned, they ignored us. We were the skeletons in their political closets, and it was expedient for their careers to put as much space between them and us as possible.

The media was rabid with a bloodthirsty feeding frenzy for the Vietnam war. At no time did the media give a single thought to spare the soldiers sent by the government, or grant them an ounce of consideration. We were defenseless and unprepared for the onslaught of hatred when we arrived home. Those who fell to media influence and were unwilling to make the distinction between not supporting a war yet still supporting those who served, were weak-minded and shortsighted.

I hugged my wife, and we headed for home. It was December of 1969, thirteen months after I'd left.

The memory of that episode has led me to thank every veteran I meet, every chance I get. I never want to see this happen to any of our men and women who have served, or who will serve in our military. Most people do not understand the price that those who serve must pay. While the families and loved ones of those veterans endured their own suffering and sacrifice, they were not *there*. They did not hear the cries of those who were dying and the last words they would ever utter before they faced eternity too soon. They did not hear their screams or see their wounds. And their dreams are not haunted at night by the memories that are forever etched in their minds. This was a monumental event in my life. We who served to defend our freedoms were never appreciated, and many were treated as criminals. While there may have been some who had an appreciation for the returning Vietnam veteran, I never saw it. We were told when we got home to only wear our civilian clothes and to put our uniforms on *after* we got to base. I felt ashamed of the protesters and the media who fed the frenzy. They never liked us and made no attempt to hide it. We were spat on and accused of being baby killers.

I never realized we were hated with such vehemence until I returned home. Many came home in body bags. Many more returned home permanently maimed, physically, mentally, emotionally and spiritually, to an ungrateful people who were clueless and apathetic to our sacrifice. I can, in any event, be grateful that my own friends and family were supportive and welcomed me home.

Years later, a beautiful memorial was finally erected in Washington, D.C. honoring those who fell in the Vietnam War. While long overdue, it is an important monument that can aid in the healing of the Vietnam veterans and the nation that so shamefully mistreated them.

I returned to the comforts of home and thirty blissful days of leave, without a single firework to celebrate. I spent time with my daughter, Jacky, whom I had not seen in over a year. It was an adjustment learning to deal with her because she no longer knew me. It didn't hurt me because I understood. Other men and women dealt with the same challenges upon their re-entry to home and family. I learned how to become her daddy, and she learned how to become my daughter. We enjoyed our leave and visited my folks. Arleen was finishing her second-grade teaching contract.

I returned home December of 1969, on a cold, dreary, snow-covered day in Indiana. My father, a WWII veteran, had seen combat in Northern Italy, France, and Germany. When I walked through the door, my dad gave me a big hug. On the third or fourth day after I returned home, he asked me to go outside and walk with him. Bundled up, we headed down the hill and sat on a swing. He and I talked for over an hour, while the wind nipped at our faces and stung our eyes.

My father belonged to a generation of men that didn't show their emotions. They had them, of course, but somewhere in their training, they became adept in the art of non-expression. Our conversation was more between two veterans than a father and son, although warmth and love were palpable.

While most of our conversation was deeply personal and too private to share, he did tell me one heartwarming story about his service in World War II. His unit was doing house-to-house reconnaissance, checking for German soldiers in a village north of Garmisch, Germany. He came upon a house and heard a noise. Pushing the door open with the barrel of his rifle, not knowing what he might find, he came upon a group of adults standing in a circle holding hands and praying. No one looked up. They just kept praying, but a small girl who was about four or five years old, looked up and waved shyly at him with a sweet smile on her face. My father said he quietly closed the door and kept moving. When he told me this story, tears streamed down his cheeks.

We discussed many other things about our experiences, but I have never shared that conversation with anyone. I would, however, as a result of that conversation, offer this valuable advice: when you thank a veteran for his service, sincerely look him in the eyes and say, "Thank you for your service." Almost inevitably, one of two things will happen. Tears will come to their eyes, or, they will simply look away. If you ask a veteran to tell their story to you, make sure you just listen or occasionally ask a question. Don't interrupt them, and you will discover the very core of the values this nation was built on, just by listening. So many times, a person will ask me what it was like in Vietnam, but when I begin to tell them, they launch into a movie they saw about the war and have decided they already know what I went through because of what they saw on the screen. At that point, I shut down and listen to their comments. They don't really want to know.

CHAPTER 10

Settling In and Moving On

Homecoming means different things to different people. When I came home from Vietnam, my outlook on life had changed. War changes a person. Before the war, I had never considered the eternal, intrinsic value of human life. I thought I had but, well, I was wrong. Now, after thirteen interminably long months of tragedy, bloodshed, sorrow, and loss, I understood how precious and fleeting life is. Whether long or short, God gives each of us the gift of one life. How we live it, is up to us. Each day is a gift of inestimable value.

The day before I left Vietnam, my executive officer, Major Murphy, said to me, "Congratulations, Lieutenant! We're crediting you with three hundred sixty-three kills." While that number reflected the body count credited to me for my kills in Vietnam, the number was nothing more than an empty victory to me. At any rate, I found it hard to believe. If it was true, then the men those numbers represented were combatants fighting for their cause, with the goal of making me die for my country. They were valiant warriors in a cause I believe was evil, but their lives were no less precious than mine. They espoused a different view of life than I did. I do not believe in Communism in any fashion. It robs a human being of dignity, worth, choice, and humanity. Communism is a destroyer of the soul. It devalues individuality to the lowest common denominator. Every part of a human being's life is dictated by a governmental system. Personal choice is never an option, and there is no freedom; not even the ability to enjoy the fruits of one's own labor. But at the end of the day, these men still fought for their country, just as I fought for mine.

In spite of my sadder but wiser outlook, my homecoming was joyous. I missed my wife and daughter more than words could ever express. And in spite of the rude and undeserved welcome I received as a veteran from fellow Americans, it was still good to be home.

After our leave, Arleen and I packed our things and headed for Cherry Point, North Carolina. While we were en route, my orders were changed to New River, North Carolina, back to my original squadron, VMO-1.

When we arrived in Jacksonville, North Carolina, we were pleased to discover that we could settle down and purchase a home, rather than rent. In February 1970, we found a small three-bedroom home, less than fourteen hundred square feet with no basement, and a big backyard. We found it amusing that our first home was located on Jackson Street in Jacksonville, North Carolina. At least the address would be easy to remember.

I was nervous and felt sick to my stomach about purchasing a new home. The house payment was $146 a month. I didn't know how we could afford such a large payment. How times have changed. The electric bill in my home today is significantly more than the amount of my first house payment!

As Arleen and I prepared to purchase this home, we got all kinds of conflicting and unsolicited advice. I was advised that if you go in and feel good about purchasing a home, then you probably could have spent a little more money and bought a larger home. If you go in and you are queasy, then you are probably just about right. But if you go in and become seriously ill, you may have gone too far in your purchase. I thought for sure I would vomit all over the agent's desk. Everyone had an opinion, and none of them were helpful.

As we were preparing to sign for the home, I told the gentleman selling the home that I couldn't buy this house because I didn't have any furniture to put in it. All the furniture we owned was a baby crib and a high chair. A panicked look came over his face at the thought of us backing out of the sale. The man's name was Itchy Hopkins. He told me if I bought the home, he would get me all the furniture I could afford at cost. Since North Carolina is one of the furniture capitols of the world and makes some of the finest furniture in the United States, we thought that sounded like a good deal, and the purchase went through.

Our new home had no air conditioning. To keep from wilting into a puddle in the North Carolina heat, we installed a wall-mounted unit between the living room and kitchen. While North Carolina had its share of humidity, nothing could compare to Vietnam. I was grateful that Vietnam was behind me and I wanted it left exactly there. The air traveled down the hall and kept the rest of the house cool. Now, all we needed were some good neighbors. That need was soon met.

John LeCave returned from Vietnam shortly after I did. Arleen and I were happy to not only be reunited with our good friends but excited that they were moving in next door to us. Susan and Arleen had met eighteen months earlier, for the first time at Pensacola Air Station Chapel. They were the only two Marine wives to pin wings on their husbands. While we didn't know it at the time, our friendship would prove to last a lifetime.

I joined the squadron again. It was a composite squadron of AH-1Gs and OV-10s. Life was different upon my return to the States. I was now a seasoned combat veteran and fully understood what was required of me. My job was to impart what I had learned to the new pilots preparing to go over.

I still loved flying and was interested in enrolling in the United States Naval Test Pilot School. When I was in Vietnam, I would wonder who wrote the textbooks for the airplanes that instructed how to start them, how to fly them, and what to do in case of emergency. I wanted to know who designed the different aircraft and why one design was chosen over another. In the heat of battle, I had to do things with airplanes that were not included in the textbooks, but they worked. For example, I had to jettison the external fuel tank. I avoided a missile by turning into it; a missile cannot make the turn. I flew fast with the nose down, which was against the instruction in the books, but by doing so, I escaped being hit. The textbooks did not include these moves, but they saved my life.

While I was in the squadron, I knew two majors, Major Jim John and Major D.E.P "Dep" Miller, who had been to the test pilot school. I asked them how they had accomplished this, and they told me about the entry requirements. Once I had my family settled, I researched the entry requirements for this school. My insatiable thirst to know more about planes had not been dimmed by the war. The sky was still calling me. I think it's hard to understand unless you're a pilot. There is a freedom in the sky that seems limitless. No traffic lanes, no stop lights, just me, my plane that soars unfettered, and God. There's a well-known poem, *High Flight*, that best explains it:

> *Oh! I have slipped the surly bonds of earth,*
> *And danced the skies on laughter-silvered wings;*
> *Sunward I've climbed, and joined the tumbling mirth*
> *Of sun-split clouds, and done a hundred things*
> *You have not dreamed of—Wheeled and soared and*
>   *swung*

High in the sunlit silence. Hov'ring there
I've chased the shouting wind along, and flung
My eager craft through footless halls of air...
Up, up the long, delirious, burning blue
I've topped the wind-swept heights with easy grace
Where never lark or even eagle flew—
And, while with silent lifting mind I've trod
The high untrespassed sanctity of space,
Put out my hand, and touched the face of God.

~ John Gillespie Magee, Jr.
1922-1941

My job in the squadron was to help the new guys going over to support the ground troops, get some back up to speed, get the new pilots ready to go into battle, and help train the maintenance people and the ground crew. This was important to me because if I failed to tell them everything I had learned, it could cost them their lives or the lives of their fellow combatants. I held nothing back, telling them everything I had learned in the hope that I would serve them the way others had served me.

In the North Carolina squadron, we had two different types of aircraft. We cross-trained with both types, teaching how to fly the airplanes, and what would be required of them in a combat situation. I needed to train them to accurately deliver the ordnance on the airplanes. We were involved in a lot of exercises with the ground combat element such as the infantry Marines, helping them learn close air support. The responsibility of properly and thoroughly training my fellow Marines was a weight I keenly bore.

In addition to other responsibilities, I was assigned to the maintenance department as one of the assistant maintenance officers. Working in the maintenance department was a valuable and educational experience. I began to learn the many details involved in the maintenance of aircraft—what was required, new parts, time on components, when they were changed out, what to do when an airplane returned with a discrepancy another pilot had found. I learned how the mechanical systems worked, and who repaired different parts of the airplane. For example, we had electricians who helped maintain the radios and the avionics in the aircraft. We had sheet metal workers who repaired broken metal, and hydraulics men who were responsible for the hydraulic system actuators, and determining when leaking hydraulic fluid or lines needed to be changed. The ordnance men handled the machine guns on the airplanes and built up the ordnance we dropped. It was a great experience and furthered my interest in the test pilot school. If this was what the mechanics entailed, my interest was piqued, and I wanted to know how to build airplanes and make them fly.

During this time, I was sent to Fort Eustis, Virginia, to an Army helicopter school for maintenance officers so I could learn how to become a good Post Maintenance Inspection Pilot. When an airplane was repaired by the ground crew, it was my responsibility to fly it to ensure the work was done correctly. Several of the aircraft required many hours of flying. There was much information to process, so I studied hard. It was a good school, and I learned much.

I also had the opportunity to attend the same type of school on the OV-10 Bronco, the twin-engine turbo-prop observation airplane that was in my squadron. Because of that experience, I was asked to be one of five people to attend Bell Helicopter, near Dallas, Texas, to pick up the new twin-engine J Model Cobra helicopter. How excited I was!

We left to pick up the first five helicopters. It was a privilege to get aircraft that had two engines. We learned how to fly them and learned their systems.

When we brought the helos back to North Carolina, I was in the original cadre of pilots who helped stand up, or organize, the first twin-engine Cobra Squadron. I was grateful for that opportunity. It wasn't all work, however, because I got to fly.

Although I worked long ten-hour days, I always made a point to be home in the evening for dinner with my family. I could never have accomplished all that was set before me without the loving support of my family, and Arleen was up for the task.

The adjustment of returning from Vietnam to a normal home life was a smoother transition than I had feared. Arleen was a rock, but at the same time, flexible, as the rigors of military life demanded. She has been my greatest blessing, a true gift from God, and I am both proud and humble to call her my wife. Adjusting to family life away from Vietnam was a welcome change for us. Arleen and I were active in our church and in the squadron. It was good to be back in church again as life returned to what I had hoped for. Our lives felt normal and happy. But I still have memories...and always will.

Early each morning, I would leave for work, carpooling with my next-door neighbor and friend, John LeCave, who was in a squadron close to mine. Our first-born had arrived shortly after theirs. We took turns driving so our wives could have a car to go to the commissary, or to take the children, who were too young for school, wherever they needed to go. We enjoyed a close friendship with John and Susan, and it was a bonus to have them as our neighbors.

John and I were promoted to captains, which, thankfully, meant a significant increase in pay. There were several of us in the squadron, but because of the war, many people were getting out of the military. Back then, we went in as reserve officers, but in an effort to keep officers in the Marine Corps, they were offered a regular commission routinely. I accepted mine. I confess I had no idea what I'd done. There were little pigeon holes against the wall in the squadron ready room that served as our mailboxes and a place where messages could be left. I found a piece of paper in my pigeon hole that said if I wanted to accept a regular commission, I should sign the paper and turn it in to Admin. Actually, I had no idea what a regular commission was, but it sounded good to have one, so I signed the paper and turned it in. Next thing I knew, I was called into the commanding officer's office, raised my right hand and was sworn in as a regular officer, thus going from a reservist to a regular officer. Promotions were quick. That gave us some breathing room and helped improve our modest lifestyle.

We'd been in Jacksonville, North Carolina about a year when our second daughter, Kathy, made her debut at a Camp Lejeune hospital which has now been converted to one of the division command headquarters. Kathy was born on December 9, 1970. We gave her the nickname of Chitzy Boom. She liked to be bounced when Arleen and I held her and sang her nickname to her. Her contagious giggle filled our home with laughter. Now we had two precious little girls. Kathy was a wonderful baby, and Jacky, at a grown-up two and a half years old, was proud of her role as the good big sister.

As we knit our family together, we found contentment. I wished Vietnam would grow to a distant memory; however, I would wake at night from the dreams that haunted my sleep. I've worked very hard to put those memories behind me. Sometimes I can, but at other times, it doesn't work. Eventually, I would shove those thoughts and feelings into a box and lock it. They can stay in the box for a long time...until someone shows up with the key. It could be a phrase, a look, an outfit, a taste, a sound or a smell. Or something unexpected. Whichever, Vietnam will, to one extent or another, be always with me.

The routines of a military family are, to say the least, interesting. Fortunately, children are adaptable little creatures. When I returned from Vietnam, and we moved to North Carolina, the movers had packed everything we owned. Arleen had taken care of all the details, as so often happens with military wives. She paid the bills, maintained the car, nurtured our daughter, and ran the household single-handedly for a year. The life of a military wife is lonely and difficult when her husband is at war. We had seen each other only five days in Hong Kong. I was proud of Arleen for keeping everything running smoothly on her own with no support. It was not an easy task, but with God to give her strength, Arleen accomplished it.

In our new home, we began to re-establish our family. Arleen turned things over to me after Kathy's birth. I would take over the duties she had so competently assumed in my absence, and Arleen would have less pressure to deal with. My most important job, however, was putting together the children's toys.

We moved numerous times, as military families do. Arleen had been given some exceptionally beautiful china as a twenty-first birthday gift from her parents, with full service for twelve. Arleen loved that china, and we still have it today. It was especially treasured because once we were married and her family distanced themselves from her, the china was the last good memory she had of them.

We lived in front of two hundred acres of open fields and a dirt road. The acreage behind us belonged to a major paper company.

One cold February day, in 1970, I was burning the wrappings and packaging from our recent move in a fifty-five-gallon trash drum, and two-year-old Jacky was with me to supervise while I burned the paper. I was holding her, keeping her away from the fire, and we were talking. When I put a stick in the fire to stoke it, I felt it hit something hard. As I continued to move the stick into the ashes, I pulled out a small salad bowl, and with a sick feeling in my stomach, I realized that while unpacking, I had inadvertently missed unwrapping a piece of Arleen's beautiful china.

Jacky looked up at me with wide eyes, and announced, "You burnt one of Mommy's good bowls!" As though I needed a reminder.

"Yes, honey, I know. Don't say anything to Mommy just yet. I'll tell her."

"Okay," she solemnly promised.

We started back toward home. About halfway to the house, Jacky took off in a dead run hollering in a clearly outdoor voice, "Mom! Dad just burned one of your good china bowls!"

So much for swearing a two-year-old tattletale to secrecy! I ran after the little blabbermouth. I was going to catch that pint-sized traitor and tickle her to no end. Arleen got to her first. After more than fifty years of marriage, I still haven't heard the end of how I burned a good china bowl. But there was an upside to this event—I knew then that Jacky recognized me and remembered me as her daddy.

It was hard to say no to my delightful daughters. I may have returned home hardened by war, but when my little darlings batted their eyes, I dissolved into goo. Boo asked for a kitty, so we got her a little gray-striped tabby, which she named Susie. Predictably, Susie grew into a cat. Cats are not as cute as kittens. But my daughter loved her, and that was all that mattered. When Boo was three years old and got into mischief, I would ask her, "Who did this?"

She would solemnly answer, "The kitty did it."

If she spilled something or got into something she wasn't supposed to, she would announce, "It did it itself."

I would tell her, "No, it didn't."

She would answer, "Susie, my kitty, did it."

How do you combat that? Americans do not negotiate with terrorists, even if they are short and adorable.

This was a precious time in our lives. I was happy to be home. We were content, and thankful for the blessing of family.

I was considering leaving the Marine Corps and returning to work for General Motors in Warren, Ohio. I thought that civilian life would be more stable and beneficial for my family. We could put down roots and enjoy the American dream. I wrote to General Motors and told them I was thinking of leaving the military and inquired as to what positions, if any, were available. About a month later, I received their reply letter stating they would be glad to have me back. The letter included a list of the available openings, with their offer to choose a position. I reviewed the list carefully, but none of the jobs appealed to me at all. I wanted to provide for my family but didn't want to take a job that I already knew I'd be unhappy working. I prayed for guidance, and once again, I felt the pull to learn how and why airplanes do what they do. I began to seriously look into attending the United States Naval Test Pilot School in Patuxent River, Maryland.

CHAPTER 11

United States Naval Test Pilot School

I had no idea that the application process to enter the United States Naval Test Pilot School was so rigorous and would involve a difficult selection process. I assumed it revolved around an ability to fly airplanes and had not given much consideration to the academic portion the school required to graduate as a test pilot.

I went to Headquarters Marine Corps in Washington, D.C. In Vietnam, I had worked with Major Don Miller, who was now in the assignments branch of Headquarters Marine Corps. Major Miller, who eventually became Major General Miller, was a close friend. We discussed the requirements necessary to get into the school. To my surprise, it required recommendations from commanding officers, a copy of my college transcript, certain academics, including heavy math and physics, as well as some chemistry and mechanics. Fifteen hundred hours of flight time were required, which I had because of my time in Vietnam, and the flying I had done in the squadron.

The process was arduous and complex. This was not the typical run-of-the-mill school to which I had become accustomed in the military. Selection for the other schools was based on an applicant's performance to-date, coupled with past history. For example, I was not allowed to attend basic school, which most Marines attended before leaving for Vietnam, nor was I allowed to go to Command and Staff School. I had to take those schools via correspondence because there was no time to send me. Therefore, when I applied for those schools, I was accepted with no additional requirements.

TPS, however, was entirely different. The selection process for this school is extremely competitive and involves rank. It took about three months to collect all the information, have my college transcripts sent to Headquarters Marine Corps, and obtain three letters of recommendation from previous commanding officers, which meant I had to track down their locations, as some were retired and had left the service. I'd had so many commanding officers, I was lucky to have remembered three of their names.

I placed all this information in a package and hand-carried it to Headquarters Marine Corps. Having set the selection process in motion, I was told I would have to apply two or three times before being selected. This was discouraging news, after having completed the many tasks just to apply. To my amazement, however, I was selected on the first application, even though I didn't think I was any more qualified than the other applicants. The school generally preferred senior captains and majors, and I had just become a junior captain less than a year earlier. I was relieved and encouraged. It looked as though God was opening this door for me.

When I received the assignment, I returned to the headquarters to thank Major Miller. He told me, "Captain Jackson, you were selected because you were dual qualified in rotary wing and fixed wing. You have the appropriate flight time and significant combat experience. We've reviewed your academic record, and I have put my name on the line for you, so if you go down there and flunk out of academics, I will personally see to it that you finish your career as an officer on a deserted island with no one else on it."

Gulp! I struggled in college.

Major Miller was dead serious. He had gone to bat for me and had gotten me selected. I couldn't thank him by failing. I took his words to heart, determined to avoid a dismal future on deserted island duty.

After my selection was approved, Arleen and I once again packed up our furniture, belongings, and children, and moved from Jacksonville, North Carolina to Lexington Park, Maryland. Jacky was three and Kathy was not quite one-year-old, and already walking.

We now had two cars. I had a small car that I drove back and forth to work, and we had a nicer family car, a 1968 Pontiac LeMans. I was excited to go to Maryland, but I had no idea of the demands that would be made on me and the time required to get through this school.

We arrived in Maryland in August 1971, and rented a house in Lexington Park, just outside the base, having sold our home in North Carolina. I contacted some people who had been to TPS, and they informed me of difficulties they encountered, not only of the demands and precision of flying but the academics. Once again, it was impressed upon me how important the academics were. They advised me to spend a lot of time studying in preparation for learning why airplanes do what they do and why they are built the way they are built. I listened politely, but I had no clue as to what they were trying to prepare me for until I had finished school.

I started school September of 1971. There were twenty-six of us in the class, but only seventeen graduated that year. I have never worked so hard at anything in all my life as I did getting through the United States Naval Test Pilot School.

On orientation day, I learned what the demands of school entailed. The school lasted eight months, during which I would learn to fly airplanes with a precision I never dreamed possible. I learned to write professionally and appropriately, and I studied academics in the technical areas of aerodynamics, flight control systems, hydraulics, and the design of these airplanes, to the extent that I would be able to write the specifications. The days consisted of a half day of academics followed by a half day of flying the aircraft.

The academics in the flight school covered more calculus in the first three weeks of the eight-month school than I had covered in two years in college. The quizzes were unmerciful. There were few breaks. I started at seven o'clock in the morning and had academics in the classroom until noon. I ate when I could. Arleen packed my lunch so I could eat at my desk.

We were divided into various groups, with seven people in my class, including two Army helicopter pilots, and Air Force Captain Greg Hite, who was not a pilot but had a Ph.D. in mechanical engineering. Greg helped me academically, and I will always be grateful for his valuable assistance. All the students and instructors helped me, for that matter, because I had not picked up a book to study since leaving college. I was a line officer and learned the skills of combat, how to command troops, and how to fly formation with airplanes. I needed their academic help and struggled immensely the first three months through school. I barely achieved a passing grade, but as I progressed, my grades began to improve. In return for their help with academics, I helped them prepare for their flights, discussing how to fly their airplanes, and what to look for in preparation for the flight to evaluate the airplane. I helped them reduce the flight data upon return. We were a team, and getting through school was a team effort.

The school had an excellent philosophy. They didn't have a class standing. There would be one fellow student that was number one, and everyone else would be number two. I never knew what my standings were, but I suspected I was near the bottom academically, and near the top for flying. Regardless, everyone in the class pulled together to help each other.

My day began at five in the morning. I would study before leaving for class, especially if there was an exam. We flew unless the flights were canceled due to weather. The rule was if you couldn't see the ground, you couldn't fly. I'd usually get home around six-thirty in the evening, eat dinner with Arleen and the girls and play with them for an hour or so after dinner. They went to bed around eight in the evening and I would return to school to study and prepare for the next day, sometimes until midnight or later. I kept this grueling schedule, day in and day out, including Saturdays. We did not have academics on Saturday, but we were studying, nonetheless, working to understand how to buy, build, and fix a better airplane for the military.

I took off Sunday mornings to go to church and enjoy a meal with my family but returned to school to study by 2:00 p.m., remaining into the evening. The instructors at the school and the commanding officers suggested we take every other Friday off for a social event, to get away from school. They understood the stress and pressure we were all going through since they had also endured the same.

We did a little socializing. The wives would mingle for a while, and by ten-thirty or eleven, many had already headed home to read and study.

My routine was brutal but consistent. I even went to school on Christmas for a few hours, because I was late in writing a report. We had to document everything we had done in our reports. Sometimes these reports were two-thirds the size of the *Yellow Pages*. But we had a saying: "Brevity and clarity, without loss of continuity." We were expected to write in a certain fashion. Sometimes, we would laugh, chit-chat, and kick back for ten minutes or so, for a brief respite, but we would then return to work.

I had to make four copies of my reports, but only one copy machine was available. In 1971, copy machines had ink that spilled everywhere, and changing the ink was a very messy project. The copier belonged to the secretaries at the school. After the students would use it the night before, it would be filthy by morning. Finally, the ladies got justifiably tired of us making a mess of the machine and complained to the commanding officer. He knew we had to use it, so we were called in and told not to leave a mess. But that wasn't good enough for the secretaries, so the skipper put a sign above the copier that read, *Students will refrain from using the secretaries' reproducing apparatus...* That sign lasted about fifteen minutes, and we never heard another word from the ladies about the use of the copy machine again!

We were expected to fly airplanes we'd never flown before. I flew a couple of helicopters, as well as fixed-wing jets for the first time. We were taken up in airplanes that had variable stability and shown what could be done with these planes. I was flying fixed wings, helicopters, and many different types of planes. We were expected to know how to handle these various aircraft because in many cases, we did not go with an instructor. When we returned, we had to reduce the flight data, evaluate the airplane, and write a report. It was a schoolhouse environment, and that meant tests—not my favorite thing. The answers to the test questions on the airplanes already in the fleet were in the aircraft flight manuals, but I had to work hard to dig out those answers. Failing a test was not an option. I was being trained to develop aircraft flight manuals on new aircraft.

Flying made the course more enjoyable for me, but the demands were still arduous. I loved flying the different types of aircraft and learning what made them work. Hard work notwithstanding, I was fascinated and hooked.

The emphasis on writing reports increased. The first page was always the hardest to write. I had to explain an airplane I'd never flown. I took a Polaroid picture of the plane I had to evaluate, which was placed on the top third of an 8x10 sheet of white paper. The people making the decision to purchase the plane for the U.S. military didn't have the time to read an entire report, so they looked at the picture of the airplane and read the summary on the front page, the same as any high-level executive of a large company would do. If the summary were accurate, then they would read the rest of the report to determine whether the data substantiated a decision to purchase the aircraft.

The reports were divided into two parts. The first part discussed performance, including how fast the airplane went, how high, and what happened when it was in the air, various weights, and the center of gravity. The second part of the report included flying qualities, such as how the aircraft flew, what kind of tail it had, the types of wings, whether anhedral (wing tips pointed down), or dihedral (wing tips pointed up) and why it did what it did. Most importantly, would the aircraft complete the mission for which it was built? All of these details had to be written in each report, because the people from the Department of Defense in Washington, D.C., used these reports to base their decision whether or not to purchase.

Graduation from TPS was a humbling experience. The Navy Lieutenant John Junek, who was number one in our class, was a good aviator and brilliant man with his master's degree in Aeronautical Engineering. I considered him a good friend. He was probably the smartest individual I've ever had the privilege of meeting, and he provided valuable assistance to me. Our class had lost some to academics, some to flying, and others who were not good writers.

We also had some foreign students attending who came from countries that were our allies. This schooling was provided to them as a courtesy from our country to theirs. They reciprocated. Our pilots also trained in Great Britain and other countries.

John and the others had helped me. They knew how hard I worked. When my name was called to go forward to receive my diploma at our graduation, everyone applauded, including my fellow classmates. They honored me, knowing how I struggled. I have never forgotten their conviction to help me, and I remain appreciative of them today. They are lifetime friends. Bill Cross became an admiral, Al Diel, a fine fighter pilot, and Barry Banks, a fellow Marine, flew F-8s. These were phenomenal men, and I was humbled to be in the same room with them. When they gave me a standing ovation, I felt a strong bond with them. I knew that wherever life took us, these people would always be my friends.

Two days after graduation, the United States Navy put us on one of their transport airplanes for a ten-day field trip to several aircraft industries, where we learned how each company built their airplanes. We toured aircraft industries in Dallas, Texas, Palmdale, California, Edwards Air Force Base, and across the ocean to England, to their test range. We went to Columbus, Ohio, Rockwell, and McDonnell Douglas in St. Louis. At each place we toured, they explained their philosophy of how and why they build airplanes. We learned everything from the engineering staff, original designs, concepts, and structural testing before the airplane flew. This field trip set the stage for what was required of a test pilot beyond academic achievement. I got my first taste of the true philosophy behind building and flying airplanes.

At this time, Arleen and I decided it was time to leave our rented home and have our own home built. We found plans for a tri-level home that we both liked a lot, and once it was finished, we moved in. Arleen quickly turned the house into a home, decorating it with her tasteful personal touches. It was our first real home, and we were looking forward to entertaining our friends.

One Sunday, we had invited several people from the First Baptist Church of Patuxent River, where we were members, over to our new home for a little party. Arleen had purchased a beautiful sconce and hung it on the wall. Now, I was just a farm boy and had never even heard of a sconce, but I thought the thing was pretty. Sunday afternoon, our house was full of our friends. I wanted to show off Arleen's latest purchase, but couldn't quite remember what it was called. Unfortunately, I got my words a little mixed up, and when I pointed to it, I said to everyone, "How do you like Arleen's beautiful new douche?"

In less than a nanosecond, the air was sucked out of the room, and the temperature fell several degrees. I wasn't entirely sure what it was I said, but I knew that whatever it was, it was wrong. Arleen stalked out of the room and into the kitchen while the ladies followed her. Most of us guys—well, we weren't exactly certain what had just happened, but we could hear the ladies laughing up a storm in the kitchen. I've never been allowed to forget that embarrassing gaffe.

Upon coming home from the field trip, Arleen and I took some leave to visit my parents, who now lived in Joliet, Illinois. As always, it was refreshing to get away, see family, and let our daughters re-connect with their grandparents. My folks came to visit us every time we got a new house, but the rest of the time, we went to visit them.

When we returned, I was assigned to my first duty station, the Weapons System Test Division, or WST. At WST, we integrated the weapons system the airplanes were going to use to make them a viable platform for national defense. I was thoroughly intrigued. I was assigned to the ordnance branch, where we checked the separation of ordnance from the new airplanes, to ensure that if it came off, it didn't strike the airplane, as this had happened in the past. We found the envelope to jettison this with, learned how the weapons system was fired with the guns and rockets, and how this was integrated to be sure it was reliable and worked as intended. My assignment was serious. The war in Vietnam still raged. Bombs were still being dropped, and new airplanes were still being built.

It was interesting work because I could fly all the different airplanes on which I had projects, or for which a new weapon had been developed. We had old ordnance on new planes and new ordnance on old planes. It had to be flown on each aircraft, and the separation had to be checked in various stages. I enjoyed this because I took off with the new weapon, also called the store, whether it was a rocket or a bomb, to see how the airplane flew with it. If I didn't have to drop my ordnance, I would see if I was able to bring it back and land. If I did, I could tell how the aircraft handled, and what the requirements were. Then, I could test the actual separation of the weapon. The airplanes contained onboard data recording systems to record airspeed, dive angle, and release angle. Cameras were installed on the airplanes to film the weapon coming off the airplane. I had a multitude of tasks.

I was happy testing. In every phase of flying, my spirits soared at least as high as my aircraft. On one particular day, I flew an F-4 Phantom, A-4 Skyhawk, A-7, and an OV-10, to learn how a new weapon we had on these aircraft flew. It was wonderful! To be able to fly several different aircraft nearly every day was a dream come true! I wrote reports, sent them to Washington, D.C., but also traveled at times to Washington D.C., to explain the results to the Navy and the Marine Corps.

One of the most dangerous maneuvers involved twelve 500-pound bombs on an F-4 Phantom. We wanted to release all of these bombs at once. The objective was to get a lot of ordnance on a target with only one pass, and we wanted to see what kind of results to expect. The parameter of this particular maneuver was a sixty-degree dive, releasing around eight to nine thousand feet above the ground. A lot takes place rolling in at a very high altitude around fifteen to sixteen thousand feet to get set up for this particular maneuver. This exercise required careful timing and concentration on my part, as these circumstances do not allow for much time.

I climbed up to the rolling-in point of thirteen thousand feet over the Chesapeake Bay. The target area was a scuttle ship called *Hannibal Target*. The area was roped off and quarantined to anyone in the Chesapeake. With the release altitude of sixty-five hundred feet, my rate of speed was very fast. I had the twelve 500-pound practice bombs on the F-4. I was to roll into a sixty-degree dive and push the bomb release button, releasing all twelve of the bombs from the airplane. We were looking for a bomb-to-bomb collision if they all came off and bumped each other, or if one came off and hit the plane. When I rolled in, I was traveling at five hundred knots. I hit the bomb release button, but none of the bombs came off. I took a quick look at the switches, and everything was set up properly. I set the bomb release again, and nothing happened. I was past my point. Now I had to recover. We had not considered what would happen if the bombs did not come off, or the altitude at which we should recover. When I started to pull the nose up, the extra weight caused the aircraft to go to an accelerated stall, and it buffeted, jerked, and kicked. I had to be very gentle with it. The ground was rushing up rapidly, and I could see the water coming up toward the airplane. The power was at idle, and I gently, but firmly, pulled the airplane around the corner and rounded it off, recovering at only eight hundred feet above the water. I returned the F-4, and a wiring problem was discovered.

I was angry that I'd missed the test point and had to do it again. I saw this as a failure and thought it made me look bad, but there was a lesson in it. I learned in my testing experience not to paint myself into a corner. Piloting is a risky business, and until this incident, most things had worked well. A test pilot's job is to reduce the risk as much as possible. I went back the next day after repairs had been made, and hit the point with no problem.

Another time, I was testing a Cobra helicopter AH-1G, to see if we could shoot 10-inch rockets off of it. This was a rush project, to be accomplished immediately. Ideally, I should have built up by shooting one or two rockets at a time, but since we were pressed for time, corners were cut. No matter what the time allowed is, however, things should be done right. I shot sixteen 10-inch rockets off the helicopter at one time. This created over-pressure on the side of the helicopter and blew the transmission doors and the engine cowling doors open; locks came loose, and doors were flapping in the breeze. Debris from the rockets peppered the tail rotor. My co-pilot, Bob Wittenberg, called me an SOB because the rockets blew the door open on his side, and he had to quickly reach out and close it. I was able to slow the helicopter and bring it back, but with significant damage. We had to come up with new ratchets and figure out how many could be shot at once. This testing experience further ingrained in me to never rush things.

I also learned that the Structures team was like black magic. I was carrying some stores of ammunition and applying G-forces to the stores. The Structures people assured me that everything would be fine. On the fifth flight, one particular store was attached by two hook points. The front hook point broke and left this store dangling in the breeze. When I landed, I showed the structural engineer. He told me he couldn't see it until after it broke, but claimed he already knew it was going to break. That infuriated me! Why didn't he tell me he knew it would break before I took off? I learned from this experience that if you are a single pilot, you're responsible for everything. If trouble ensues, or anything changes, you must take care of it. The ground crew is only as good as the data they receive. They'll respond to that, but sometimes the response time is so quick, they can't analyze it, and it falls back on the pilot.

Of course, as in all aspects of the military, we had our share of humorous moments, bombs and danger notwithstanding. One time, the Secretary of the Navy came to Patuxent River to view the facility, and we decided to impress him with a mighty demonstration of firepower. One of my friends was flying in this demonstration, and I was asked to be a part of it by shooting rockets. Test airplanes are not wired the way fleet airplanes are. They are wired for experimental testing. I had the switches right, but the aircraft was wired wrong! I was in an A-4 Skyhawk, and instead of shooting eight rockets, I jettisoned four rocket pods into the bay. The Secretary of the Navy's wife, also in attendance, chuckled and commented, "I sure hope we're not using that to win the war." I learned of her comment but cleared my good name by proving that the wiring was wrong.

Another funny incident occurred regarding the admiral's reserved parking spot at the Officer's Club.

I normally did not attend the happy hours on Friday night, preferring to get home to my family. One night, there was a going-away party for a good friend of mine who was leaving the service and returning to Iowa to work on his family farm. He was looking forward to going back to civilian life, and I wanted to wish him well. As I drove around the Officer's Club on this Friday evening, there was only one parking space left. It belonged to Admiral Isman. It appeared the admiral would not be coming because it was around 6:00 p.m. I figured I would just run in quickly and say goodbye to my friend, and no one would ever know that I had parked briefly in his spot. I was at the club for about half an hour, when suddenly, two big military police, Shore Patrol, approached me and asked if I was Captain Jackson. I told them I was and asked what was wrong, and what they wanted. I was rather indignant.

They asked, "Would you step outside?"

I asked them, "What for?"

They told me to just step outside. I did and saw the problem.

Admiral Isman's car was parked right behind mine. There was no way to get out. As I came out, I snapped a salute and came to attention. The admiral said, "Captain, be in my office at 7:30 a.m., Monday morning." My heart sank. He moved his car, and I got in mine and went home.

I told Arleen about the situation. I envisioned everything from a letter of reprimand to a firing squad, as I worried the entire weekend about what might happen. I shined my shoes, got a haircut and polished my brass. I practiced my speech in the mirror on Sunday afternoon. It was something like, "Yes sir, I will never let it happen again."

The admiral had instructed me to arrive at his office on Monday at 7:30 a.m., so at 7:10, I was already present. The admiral's secretary, a gracious lady, had been an admiral's secretary for twenty years or more, and she told me to have a seat. I could hear that the admiral was in his office by the rustling of papers. At 7:25, I began to stand and be prepared, but 7:25 became 7:30, then 7:45, lasting into eternity.

Finally, his secretary came out. "Captain Jackson, the admiral will see you now."

I walked in and stood at attention. I never looked him in the eye and stared straight out the window. In the military, you just stand at attention, staring straight ahead, and only speak when spoken to. I entered and snapped to attention.

"Captain Jackson reporting as ordered, sir."

The admiral was not a tall man, but he was stocky. He slowly looked up from his desk. I could not see what he was doing. Finally, he said, "At ease." I stood at ease. He took his glasses off and laid them on his desk. "Captain, I have been in the Navy thirty-two years, and this is the first time in my entire life I have had my own parking spot. Now, will you stay out of it?"

Without hesitation, I replied, "Yes, sir."

He began to laugh. "I think I've made my point."

"Yes, sir, you have."

In that instant, the whole scene changed in his office. He smiled and invited me to have a seat in a chair. The office was furnished with a couch and chair with coffee tables between them. It was a bright Monday morning, and the sun was shining. It looked like I was going to live after all. The admiral sat down beside me and asked his secretary to bring us coffee. I wondered what would transpire now. I felt the parking situation had passed, and I had learned my lesson. So, now what?

The admiral began, "Jack, I've heard about you, and I've heard you're doing a lot of flying in my test center. When you're at the top, sometimes people tell you what you want to hear, and not what they are hearing. What's going on at my test center? Tell me what you see."

For the first time, I saw in a flag officer what I have
since seen so many times in general officers in the Marine Corps, regardless of the rank they hold, be it one
star or four. I saw the true character of a flag officer
in the military. They cared more about the men, the
equipment, and the nation than I had realized. Here,
in the admiral's office was a young officer talking to
a senior officer in command. The admiral absorbed
the things I told him, whether good or bad. I learned
a long time ago, not to take a problem to your boss
without a solution. I told the admiral the problems I
saw, and how I thought they could be fixed. Whether
he chose to incorporate my suggestions remained to
be seen. Our conversation lasted about an hour. After
that, we became good friends.

I eventually lost track of Admiral Isman and his
lovely wife. Mrs. Isman and Arleen became friends
and headed the fundraising for the Navy Relief Program for struggling Sailors and Marines on the base.

Before we left Patuxent River Naval Air Station,
we were invited to dinner at the Isman's home. We
were treated well, and he set an example for me as to
the behavior and attitudes of someone with high-rank-
ing authority. I have since seen that in generals and
others, but this was my first one-on-one encounter
with a flag officer. This opportunity had been a good
learning experience. I learned that when you attained
a certain position, getting your next rank or next promotion is no longer the most important goal. What
matters most are the people in your organization.

Another lesson I learned, even if temporarily, was
not to smart off. You'd think I would've remembered
this from my youth, but I confess to being a bit of a
smart aleck as an adult. While I had developed a new
respect for the officers I dealt with, sometimes, as a
young officer, I relapsed.

One day, I was doing a required maintenance inspection flight for an A-4 Skyhawk. On my return from testing the aircraft, I put the landing gear down and heard a loud bang on the side of the airplane. At first, I thought it was an engine surge, like a backfire from a car. It came behind me from the left side, as I was preparing to land. I first looked at the engine, and it was still working. I checked to see if the landing gear was down, and noticed I was losing hydraulic pressure. I made a full-stop landing right away, taxied clear, and shut down the airplane.

The safety officer, a Navy lieutenant commander, and senior to me, came running and asked, "What happened? What happened?"

I answered, "Well, sir, I put the landing gear down, and there was a loud bang. I thought the engine surged. I tried to eject. The ejection seat didn't work, so I landed." Before I could tell him I was joking, he turned and raced back to file his report that way. It took me forever to get this sorted out, and the man never forgave me. I was only making an attempt at humor but learned some things, or at the least, some people, shouldn't be dealt with lightly.

My testing experience also took me to Washington, D.C., where I learned procurement operations. I was evaluating three different gun sights made by three different companies. When we picked the winner, one of the company representatives who had lost filed a complaint, which they had the right to do. This complaint went all the way to a Sub-Armed Forces Committee Hearing. I was called into the office with the other senior officers because I had flown the aircraft, and they were describing it. Finally, a member of Congress turned to me and asked, "Captain Jackson, what do you think of this system?"

I was unsure of the best way to respond.

He pressed on, "Can we win the war with this system?"

I answered, "Sir, we can win the war with the one I picked. The other two aren't as good, and they won't help us win the war."

The congressman sat down and announced the decision was now final.

As I walked away, the congressman asked me if I had a minute.

I thought, Oh, no, here we go.

When the other senior officers moved in closer to me, the congressman waved them off and said, "No, just you." The senior officers who had accompanied me for support left the room.

The congressman told me he was a former Marine, and we began to chat about the Marine Corps, who we knew, who was flying, who was on the ground, and what had become of certain individuals. He was before my time, but I still remembered some of the officers. It was an interesting conversation. As I left the office, he smiled and said, "Captain, *Semper Fidelis*," the term Marines use which means we are always faithful to one another, as well as to our nation. Once again, I felt the pride of the Marine Corps.

CHAPTER 12

The Society of Experimental Test Pilots

One of the benefits of getting through TPS is to become a member of an organization called The Society of Experimental Test Pilots. I'm a lifetime member of the SETP organization. To attain membership, I needed to have tested airplanes, flown aircraft where someone else has never flown and tested where someone else has never tested. At the test center in Maryland, I had the opportunity to participate in envelope expansion, to test new weapons systems and new airplanes. I qualified to become a member of SETP, and eventually became an Associate Fellow.

Every September, SETP conducts two small and one main symposium. Technical papers are presented at the main symposium from all branches of the service, and from all industries on what is being done, where, and available programs. The first year I was accepted as a member, I attended the main symposium. I took Arleen with me, and we splurged for airline tickets. The event was held at the Hilton Hotel in Beverly Hills, California.

We had never attended anything of this magnitude. There was a conference presenting technical papers on Friday, with a poolside reception Friday night. Saturday morning through the afternoon, more technical papers were presented, followed by a luncheon with a guest speaker. In the evening, a formal, black-tie dinner was held where awards were presented to the test pilots who had achieved an outstanding accomplishment in testing, aviation, and technical writing for that year. Some of the years I attended, Bob Hope was the Master of Ceremonies. Former Secretary of Defense Caspar Weinberger attended one year. Well-respected people were chosen as the Master of Ceremonies, and they always did a wonderful job.

The first year I attended, however, I did not know the banquet tickets were hard to get, and should have been ordered months in advance. Arleen wore her formal gown, and I, my Marine dress blues. When I tried to purchase tickets, none were available. We were placed on standby. While we were standing around waiting, I said to Arleen, "Let's go get some dinner."

We went to the hotel restaurant and met a couple dining. The gentleman was a wealthy businessman from Los Angeles. He and his wife were eating dinner, and when he saw us, he said, "Captain, what brings you up here?"

I replied, "Sir, my wife and I planned to attend the banquet, but I couldn't get tickets. We're on standby."

The gentleman rose, left the table, and returned with two tickets for us. I do not know how he got those tickets, but we thanked him and got his address so that we could send him a formal thank-you note. I later learned he was a major car dealer in Los Angeles. This was one of the rare times that as a veteran of the Vietnam War, someone treated me well. We graciously thanked them and attended the banquet. I wish I could remember this dear gentleman's name. So many years have gone by since that first symposium, but I still remember his kind gesture.

When we arrived, everyone was already seated, and they were beginning to serve dinner. The waiter took our tickets, and I assumed we would be in the back of the room. There were one thousand to fifteen hundred people in attendance. The waiter weaved us through the crowd, from the second level to the first level, down to the main floor. We were almost near the front when I saw the only two empty seats available. I immediately recognized Chuck Yeager seated at the same table. I let Arleen sit next to him, and I took my seat beside an elderly lady. I was stunned to learn she was Jackie Corcoran! Jackie Corcoran has since passed away, but she went down in the annals of aviation history as one of the first women pioneers to fly airplanes during World War II. She was an icon in women's aviation, and I had the privilege as a young Marine captain to sit next to her at this banquet. Chuck Yeager was very kind to Arleen and me, as well as the entire table. These celebrities must have realized we were in awe of them and may have sensed we felt somewhat out of place seated at this table. It was a wonderful event for our introduction to The Society of Experimental Test Pilots. I have since seen Chuck Yeager at subsequent events. Although we are not close friends, I have gotten to know him, and have become more appreciative of what he has done for aviation.

I have presented a paper or two at the symposiums, as well. Not long ago, I had the honor of being one of the guest speakers. I'm proud to be associated with such a wonderful organization. Although Arleen and I attended many times, that first wide-eyed trip was our most memorable.

CHAPTER 13

The Final Separation

Four years passed. We were still living in Patuxent River, Maryland when a most significant event occurred. On a hot August day in 1974, we were blessed to welcome our third child, Jeff, as the fifth member of our family. Jeff was a large baby, born almost a month late. The birth of our son, whose nickname is Tiger Joe, completed our family and was the highlight of my Patuxent River time there. Even though he now has children of his own, Arleen still accuses Jeff of enjoying the good life before he made his entrance into this world since she carried that child ten months.

We enjoyed happy, content family life, were members of a great church and blessed with dear friends while we lived there. Testing was demanding, yet fulfilling. When testing, I received instant feedback on my flying performance, hitting the data point in the sky, and evaluating the airplane. This was a time of deep joy and gratitude for our family, church and social life, and my career. It was one of the happiest times in my life. But it would not last long.

I received an assignment to the Western Pacific, or West Pac, as Marines call it. This would be an unaccompanied tour, and once again, Arleen would be left to run our home alone, now with three children.

The Vietnam War had finally come to an end. My time in the States was up, and now I, like so many other members of our military, had to return overseas to extend the long arm of defense of our country.

I left Arleen and the children in Maryland, in the tri-level home we had designed and built over four years ago. We thought it was best they stayed there, because Jacky, our oldest, was now in school. We didn't want to disrupt their lives more than necessary.

The hardest part of this deployment was leaving Arleen and the three children. My son, Jeff, was only eight weeks old. I had to say goodbye, and everybody cried. While the joys of the squadron were rewarding in many aspects, the separation from my family was beginning to take its toll.

Arleen was and is a strong, competent woman and an excellent military wife. I don't believe military wives ever get the credit they deserve. They must manage all the affairs of the household and rear the children while dealing with their fears and challenges alone. They must perform miracles on a limited budget, and often feel isolated. They are women of courage and faith, a special breed, whom I hold in the highest esteem. The tears shed when I got out of the car at Dulles Airport tore my heart. I wondered if leaving them was the right decision, but Arleen and I had prayed, asking God for wisdom and guidance, and this was the direction we believed we were to take. But it certainly wasn't easy.

I left for Iwakuni, located in the Nishiki River delta of southern Japan where I joined the fighter squadron, VMFA-232, in November 1974, for a thirteen-month tour. This time, we did not expect any combat to be involved, as we were pulling out of Vietnam. In Iwakuni, I was the assistant maintenance officer and flew the F-4 Phantom Fighters. As a captain, it was always a pleasure to meet the squadron. I was looking forward to making major.

While serving as an assistant maintenance officer and having the opportunity to fly every day was a pleasure, a seed was planted in my heart, impressing upon me that there was more to life than being in the military, and being stationed overseas without my family. God was beginning to polish some rough edges in my life, and the chafing was becoming uncomfortable. He was preparing me to serve elsewhere.

While I was in Iwakuni, we did tactical training. We deployed about every two months from Iwakuni to Subic Bay on the west coast of the island of Luzon in the Philippines, about sixty-two miles northwest of Manila Bay, and then went on to Korea for exercises. Our squadron moved around every sixty days to different locations for new and different training. My job was to ensure all the troops and airplanes reached our destinations, so we could fly and continue training. The jets were difficult to maintain, and we did a tremendous amount of flying. We dropped practice bombs in the area, but no live ammunition. The camaraderie of the squadron was high. Still, I missed my family.

In the summer of 1975, following Iwakuni, we deployed to Okinawa, Japan for sixty days.

Arleen and the children flew from Maryland to Okinawa to spend six unforgettable weeks with me. My children have stories they still tell of how Jacky, who was seven years old at the time, had to change American dollars to Yen, and hail taxis on the base to get to and from the base playground and library. She always took Kathy with her. While we were there, I taught Jeff to walk at ten months of age. When the first typhoon came ashore, we had to hunker down in the bachelor officers' building.

Once we were settled, we moved to a village. The Marines would not sanction dependents coming over for line officers and air wing officers. It was supposed to be an unaccompanied tour, so we rented a place in town. I would go to the base and do my job, then come home in the afternoons to spend time with my family. The kids learned to love Kobe beef, which made a delicious meal. We learned to eat with chopsticks, and Jeff celebrated his first birthday there. Kathy, being younger, didn't have as many memories as Jacky, who turned eight on that trip, but we all had a good time as a family, and I was sad when they had to leave.

In April, Arleen called me and told me it was necessary for me to return home. I'd been overseas for about seven months. She didn't tell me at that time what was so important that I was needed at home, but I managed to get a week's leave and made my way back to the States. If Arleen needed me home, I would get there any way I could.

I boarded a bullet train in Iwakuni, to go to Tokyo for my flight to the United States. The bullet train traveled at speeds of one hundred twenty miles per hour. I sat down next to an Asian gentleman, but we did not speak to each other. As we neared Tokyo, less English was spoken, and more Japanese, which I didn't understand at all. The conductor came and spoke to me in Japanese. I had no idea what he said. Since I could not understand the conductor, I turned to the Asian gentleman sitting next to me and asked him, "Do you speak English?"

In clear and perfect English, he replied, "Yes I do, but I'm from Hawaii, and I don't understand a word this gentleman says."

We finally realized that the conductor wanted our tickets.

The crisis that so desperately required my presence was that Arleen was turning thirty and did not want to celebrate her thirtieth birthday alone. I didn't see what the emergency was. I had turned thirty a couple of years before Arleen, and it was no big deal. I didn't quite understand this chink in her usually strong armor, but I was glad to come home and be with her.

After Arleen's birthday, I rejoined my squadron and we immediately left for the Philippines and began to build up carrier landing practices to go aboard the

USS Enterprise in Subic Bay. After we got there, we learned during our brief that the fall of Saigon was imminent. The Navy's F-14 Tomcat aircraft were experiencing engine problems which caused them to be grounded. Instead, we took a composite Marine squadron of F-4s, made up of VMFA-232 and VMFA-115; V for fixed wing and MFA for Marine Fighter Attack to fill in until the Tomcats were returned to flight status.

We returned to the ship in the Philippines. When she sailed, we went out and did our carrier qualifications.

It was quite an experience for me to bring a Phantom aboard the *USS Enterprise*. It was my first landing aboard a nuclear carrier, which I consider a national treasure. The nuclear carriers were battle ready and practically invincible, capable of providing firepower on land and sea with their aircraft. The battle group was magnificent. Over five thousand men and women are aboard these floating cities. I could take off and land, day or night, in any weather. This required even more precision than described earlier when I went through the training command because it involved bringing a 56,000-pound airplane aboard. The carrier qualifications, or qualls, for short, provided me with a great sense of satisfaction; not because we were capable of getting aboard the carrier, but because we were part of a battle group that was ready to go to war. Sobering thoughts of war and the reality of what could happen floated through my mind.

We moved every sixty days. After the Philippines, we returned to Japan.

This tour in the West Pac opened my eyes to the Far East and other parts of the world. As a maintenance officer, I traveled to Taiwan, where the U.S. Government had placed a rework facility for our airplanes. I learned about diplomatic relations between Taiwan and China, and about the Philippines and Manila, and the closing of the various bases located there, such as Subic Bay and Clark Air Force Base, Manila.

I took some time off and traveled to Nagasaki and Hiroshima to see the memorials. In Korea, I went to Osan, Kwangju, and Seoul, the capital of Korea, to see how the people were progressing, and how they lived. I had worked with the Korean Marines in Vietnam and understood how well they were trained. I fully understood the very real threat of North Korea at the time, which now, as I write this, pales in comparison.

I realized on this tour, how blessed we are in the United States. I thank God every day for this great nation and the freedoms we enjoy. I am willing to pay the price, whatever that price may be, to keep our country free.

The West Pac tour was a learning experience, both for my family and for me. However, I cannot say it was enjoyable. When my year was up, I was grateful to be home.

CHAPTER 14

The Harrier AV-8A

Returning home was fabulous! Opening the door to my beautiful wife waiting to hug me, and three fantastic children clambering to be picked up and hugged is the warmest, most satisfying feeling in the world. Nothing can compare to being surrounded by a loving family after both you and they have been counting the days until homecoming.

I received orders to go to Cherry Point, North Carolina, specifically, Havelock North Carolina, to begin AV-8 Harrier training. Once again, we would be moving. I was now a captain, and because of my rank, and having a wife and three children, our family was eligible for base housing. We'd never lived on base before. We sold our home in Maryland, and once again, prepared for another move. Moving is never easy. The longer you live in one place, the more stuff you collect. The more stuff you collect, the more stuff you move, and the more you move your stuff, the more your stuff gets broken. But here we were again, packing up and moving.

We left Maryland caravanning on a bright, sunny day in the winter of 1975, for the seven to eight-hour drive to our new home in North Carolina. I had the two girls with me, and Arleen took Jeff in our other car. When we arrived, we stayed in a motel the first couple of nights because our stuff had not yet arrived. I checked in at the base, pleased to be starting AV-8 Harrier training. We soon moved into base housing and were fortunate to have a small, three-bedroom home on a cul-de-sac.

Our home was comfortable. I bought carpet and laid it myself in the children's bedrooms because they had hardwood floors. We purchased a large dining room set from Itchy Hopkins, of Jacksonville—the same person from whom we'd gotten our first appliances and furniture years before!

The previous owners had closed off part of the garage, and we used that as a family room. All I had to do was buy a space heater. We had our TV out there for the kids. Base housing did not include dishwashers, so I splurged and bought a portable dishwasher. Every time we used it, we had to slide it over to the corner of the tiny kitchen, hook up the hose to the faucet, and hook the drain hose back into the sink. The first day we hooked up the washer and dryer, the kitchen flooded. The house, which had been empty for some time, was bordered by the woods, and sticks and leaves had worked their way into the plumbing system, causing the water to back up! It took base maintenance three days to get the repairs done. We had no microwave and no extras, but the fact that we were together made living anywhere joyful.

The neighbors who lived on our cul-de-sac at the end of the street were the Ogelines, Savages, and Gillilands. They were fine people who became successful in their Marine Corps careers. They were all majors or senior majors and were kind to Arleen and me, including us in their many activities. When we moved in, they brought over home-baked brownies and cookies. Some of the older girls babysat our children when Arleen and I had functions to attend with the squadron. This kind of friendship wasn't only extended in the Marine Corps because of the close bonds we share, but it set an example for me of how I should treat others who moved into our neighborhood. Neighborhood friendships and gestures are important in our society. We've gotten away from this for a while, but I believe it's coming back. The importance of caring for others took on a deeper meaning in Cherry Point, North Carolina.

Social events were in accordance with the military's schedule. If there were a change of command in a squadron from one commanding officer to another, there would always be a reception at the Officer's Club. There was Friday night happy hour, which I rarely attended because I still didn't drink. I'd seen most of these guys all week long and preferred to spend as much time with my family as possible. If there weren't a reception on Friday night, Arleen and I would take the kids out for dinner or to a family movie. We enjoyed spending time with our children, playing board games and reading to them.

The girls, now ten and seven years of age, were in school. Jeff was four. Arleen took them to their first day of school each year. Every night I'd have them sit down and tell me what they did, and sometimes help them with their homework. They would show me a new word they'd learned, or sing a song. It was more of a blessing to me than it was to them.

I was content. Life took on an importance that I never realized, or maybe I had lost it in the stress of Vietnam. I was beginning to feel again, to be able to relax. I would never and could never forget Vietnam, but the effects of combat on my soul and psyche were losing their edge. I could feel the roughness of the tightly woven shield around my heart softening, as the war became more distant. It would never leave me completely, but it was affecting my daily life and activities less as time went on.

Military social life and change of command held new meaning. The changes of command in Vietnam were informal. We stood in flight suits, the flag was passed, and then we went on to fly our combat missions. If a pilot was scheduled to fly that day, then he was unable to attend the ceremony. When I returned home, the tradition was upheld, especially for those assuming or being relieved of command after their time was up. Change of command expanded with rank. A change of command for a squadron only affected the members of the squadron itself, which comprised approximately two hundred fifty men and women; for the entire aircraft wing it was about a thousand men and women.

There was one event where one wing commander was being changed for another. A wing commander holds the same rank as a two-star general, a major general. This ceremony was in July, and North Carolina is *hot* in July. I stood in formation, with hundreds of troops out on the sweltering flight line. The temperature must have been ninety-five degrees with high humidity. It was sticky and uncomfortable. A four-star Navy admiral had come from Norfolk to be the CO, preside over the ceremony, and give a speech for this change of command. We were standing outside while our special guests had a shelter. Most of the spectators were standing out in the sun. All the seats were taken.

The admiral stood up for his speech, which was expected to last fifteen to twenty unbearable minutes. He addressed the crowd. "Ladies and gentlemen, I have prepared a speech, but it's very hot out here, so I'm going to forego that."

He turned to the general who was giving up the command and said, "You have done a very good job. Best of luck to you on your new assignment."

He then turned to the general who was taking command and said, "Congratulations on your command. Command well." Then he sat down. That took a forty-five-minute change of command ceremony down to around fifteen minutes. The troops passed in review and everyone had the afternoon off.

I've heard a lot of speeches in my time, most of which I can't remember, but that is one I'll never forget. Eventually, I would use this simple lesson when giving speeches during my political career. Get to the point and keep it short!

Harrier training was different when I started, from what it is today. I went to the VMAT-203 Squadron, where there were A-4s. They were training fixed-wing people. There were about twenty single-seat AV-8A Harriers brought in from British Aerospace. The early Harrier pilots' experience in learning to fly the plane was challenging. First, there was no two-seater. We started flying in a single seat airplane by ourselves from the first flight. The Marine Corps bought one hundred and seven AV-8As, and they had already started one squadron. The Marine Corps bought the concept of the VSTOL, a Vertical Short Take Off and Landing, but they bought an airplane that didn't have the capability they wanted concerning its weapons system. They wanted to prove the concept and improve the airplane. With a wingspan of approximately twenty-five feet, the AV-8A was difficult to fly.

The Marine Corps knew this airplane didn't meet all its needs, but it gave us a tremendous capability to help the Marine carrying a rifle, as well as the ground combat element because we could be with them every step of the way.

As I checked into the squadron, knowing that the aircraft had some deficiencies, and knowing a different type of flying would be required of me, I took a different approach to flying this plane. It was incumbent upon me to study on my own. There was no simulator like there is today. The only training information we had were the books, but they had taken a throttle quadrant from an older airplane that had crashed and put it on a board that was two feet long and twelve inches wide. You could set it on the seat next to you in the ready room to practice going from the nozzles to the throttle and removing the stow stop, which is set

for takeoffs and landings. Procedures had to be practiced with the left hand because a Harrier pilot's left
hand is busy. That has since been corrected, and the
new Joint Strike Fighter has taken that concept even
further. But at that time, it was required.

We also learned that the British philosophy of designing airplanes was different from that of the Americans; not bad, just different. For instance, most airplanes have a gear handle in the cockpit. It is shaped
like a little landing wheel and is moved up and down
to raise and lower the gear. But the British landing
gear was raised and lowered by pushing a button. One
button raised it, and another button lowered it. The
AV-8A did not have a full flight envelope stability augmentation system. The stability augmentation system
ended at two hundred fifty knots, and after that speed,
you had to physically fly the airplane. I was used to the
luxury of a system that worked as an auto-pilot, but
with the British design, I had to learn how to fly this
plane without the benefit of an auto-pilot.

I was doubly blessed in my line of work. Flying airplanes, and especially, being a test pilot did more than
provide me with a great amount of job satisfaction—
it was just plain fun! You know immediately how well
you've done in your effort to achieve your goal. You
don't have to wait for a final report to come out. You
don't have to wait to see if the deal is closed. You know
right then and there. That type of job satisfaction has
kept me in aviation to this day. There's a satisfaction
in loving what you do that is uplifting, and I believed I
was born to fly airplanes.

Our training commenced. We were assigned a pilot who had already been checked out, and the original
pilot went to England to be checked out and evaluate
the plane there. They came back, became instructors, and taught new pilots. That was how they grew
the community. After we'd gone through the ground

schools, and the instructors taught us about the systems and the airplane, we began to fly.

It was exciting to take part in bringing a totally new concept to military aviation, especially when it is still used today. Before the Harrier, the only manned aircraft that could hover was a helicopter, and helicopters were used to teach you how to hover. I started the Harrier, and went up and down, never taking off, just to see its powerful acceleration. Then I added the throttle; the airplane just accelerated. That helped with the understanding that the Harrier had to have a better than 1:1 thrust to weight ratio so I could hover. That meant a tremendous amount of thrust needed to be managed. It's quite a rush! I have not flown an airplane before or since with that type of quick, instantaneous acceleration.

The next thing we learned was how to hover. My first flight in an AV-8A was the hover. The procedure was to man my airplane while my instructor was in a pickup truck that had been fitted with radios to give me instructions on how to hover. We had a standard joke that if you were in the airplane hovering for the first or second time, saw the backup lights come on in the pickup truck, and heard the instructor holler, "Throw your wallet out," they always laughed and said you were about to crash. Joking aside, it was serious business learning how to hover this airplane, which was difficult just to fly.

The first concept to master was to go out over the hover pad and through the pre-takeoff procedures. When they were completed, I was given the go-ahead to hover. I moved the nozzles into position and added the power. My first hovers were early in the morning when it was cool, and there was plenty of performance to accomplish three or four hovers, and up I went. I was supposed to stop at fifty feet. I remember getting to about seventy-five feet, and I saw first hovers go as high as two hundred feet before the pilots got the power under control. We were in awe of the capability of the machine and hovering ability. The power and the thrill were enough to satisfy any adrenaline junkie. I got to seventy-five feet and had to look to see where I was because a hover is different than flying on instruments inside the cockpit. I spent a lot of time looking outside, picking up the visual cues and looking for movement. Sitting up there in my first hover, I thought, Okay, God, if you can get this thing down, I believe I can handle the next one. I landed and taxied clear. The airplane needed to be cooled down before the next flight. It was a euphoric feeling. I had six flights before I ever had an hour of flight time, because of practicing the hover.

The next thing we learned was the transition. The most difficult thing to do in aviation when using a VSTOL is to make the transition from the hover to conventional flight, then back from conventional flight to the hover for the landing. The theory was to very slowly move the nozzles that projected the airplane from the hover position to conventional flight, and then the Harrier could be flown like a regular airplane. After that, the nozzles were brought in slowly to come back to a position where the aircraft hovered over the pad at fifty feet, to complete the vertical landing. I had about ten flights, and that was the first evolution. From there, things developed into the normal training we had received in flight school, which we had seen in our tactical airplanes, instrument training, formation flying, dropping bombs, and shooting the guns. All these steps brought me up to speed as a combat aviator. But, I never, ever, came back with extra gas. I used it all to practice in the VSTOL modes every chance that was available.

The Harrier was not only a tricky and difficult airplane to fly, but it also came with one deeply alarming statistic. Out of the one hundred seven AV-8s that were brought to prove the concept, fifty-six had crashed, killing twenty-seven Marines. There were numerous crashes and repairs. The loss of life was staggering and tragic. Things could get out of hand so quickly, it was imperative to be vigilant at all times.

A local CBS station wanted to do a television show about the new AV-8 Harrier the Marine Corps had purchased. Senior Colonel Jim Orr requested that I appear as a junior officer to speak about the training required to fly this complicated aircraft. I was thrilled, naturally, and appeared as a guest on the show. The colonel spoke of the acquisition of the Harrier and how it would fit into the Marines' battle plan, and I commented, "Marine Harrier pilots are a breed apart."

It was intended to be an innocent statement because I was only referring to the extra workload that had to be completed with the left hand to coordinate the throttles and the nozzles, but the Marine Corps aviation community misunderstood my intention and was up in arms. "What makes you think you are any better than the rest of us?" "We have jobs." And on and on. The brouhaha went as far as Three-Star General Tom Miller. General Miller was the father of the Harrier, and responsible for getting it into the Marine Corps. He gave me priceless advice that not only made a huge difference to my career in the Marines and my career as a test pilot but especially to my later career as an elected official for the state of Missouri. When I explained my comment to the general, he said, "Let me tell you something. First of all, always remember the media is trying to sell their newspaper or television product. Second, if you *can* be misquoted, you *will* be misquoted." I took his valuable advice to heart, and I'm glad I did so.

I completed basic aircraft training and was assigned to VMA Detachment 513A. This detachment consisted of six aircraft and six pilots. There was a demand for the airplane to explore the different ways it could be used against fire aircraft. The demand then was just as great as it is today for air shows. It's a thrilling crowd pleaser, displaying the concept and capability of the Marines. This detachment was put aside to train air combat maneuvering, to do air shows, and to qualify ships with carrier landings, which allowed the regular gun squadrons to train in other areas so they would be a combat-ready unit.

The detachment CO was Major Drax Williams, who later became Major General Williams. I made other friends, flew a lot and learned much in this squadron. I learned about the VSTOL and its combat capabilities. It was a fantastic experience. I was the executive officer for Major Williams' group. This gave me the ability to not only lead but to manage the detachment from a perspective which expanded the managerial skills I used when I became a test pilot for the Boeing Company.

CHAPTER 15

End of an Era and The Beginning of a New Chapter

While at Cherry Point, my career took an unexpected turn. I was reading the message traffic one day and learned a position was available as an aide to Major General Victor Armstrong on the base. Major General Armstrong had a brilliant career in the Marine Corps. A man I held in high esteem, he was a Marine's Marine. I applied to become his Aide-de-Camp and was thrilled when I was selected.

This position meant I would be spending less time in the cockpit as a captain, but I would still fly. I learned how the Marine Corps was run from General Armstrong; the inner workings from the general officer level to the commandant. I also learned how senior officers think, act, and respond. This was my introduction to how the corporate world ran, which, unbeknownst to me, was in my future. Being the general's aide taught me protocol.

General Armstrong was a distinguished Marine and a fascinating individual. He spoke fluent Japanese, having grown up as the son of missionaries in China and Japan. He flew in the Black Sheep with Pappy Boynton, the famed World War II Marine aviator, and was a helicopter pilot in Korea. As a lieutenant colonel, he was the commanding officer of the Presidential Helicopter Squadron, HMX1, and had the distinct privilege of flying former Presidents Eisenhower, Kennedy, and Nixon.

When I became General Armstrong's aide, he was the commanding general of Marine Corps Air Bases, Eastern Coast. As his aide, my job was to ensure that the schedules were correct and the general was on time. I was responsible for the details of his transportation and events. I also had help from his executive assistant and his chief of staff. We took care of the condition of the bases, including the barracks, commissaries, and exchanges, and helped the Marines in the fleet Marine force prepare for war, if necessary. I was in the background making sure the general was in the forefront.

Once I earned General Armstrong's confidence, he began to teach me things about the Marine Corps and include me in events that normally I would not have had the opportunity to attend. With an upgraded clearance, I was able to view places in the Pentagon that most people had no clearance to enter. At times, I was in the office when the senior general officers of the Marine Corps held meetings. I met distinguished visitors to the base, including former President Jimmy Carter. Talk about benefits! General Armstrong showed me how to be an executive, a commander, and how to lead. He taught me the difference between leadership and management. I was like a sponge, soaking up every bit of wisdom and advice I could hold.

As a young captain of thirty-five, I learned that when general officers enter a room to discuss problems and find solutions that involve a concern about their organization—in this case, the Marine Corps—rank didn't matter; the goal was to find a solution to the problem. Later, when I was a test pilot attending meetings for the Boeing Company, I observed senior executives such as Sandy and John McDonnell, put the prestige that came with their rank and salary aside to dwell on the issues and problems presented, and to find workable solutions.

No one was allowed to enter General Armstrong's office, including Mrs. Armstrong, during working hours unless I brought them in. One day, a man in a flannel shirt and jeans burst through my office, straight into the general's office, and announced, "Hey, Vic, I need a jeep." I hurried in behind him, not knowing whether he was a threat, a kook, or what.

I heard the general ask, "Well, Pappy, what do you need a jeep for?"

The man was none other than Pappy Boynton!

He answered, "I need a jeep to get to Washington, D.C. My car's broken down."

General Armstrong told him he couldn't give him a government vehicle. Pappy Boynton was obviously out of the service. I was excited about the chance to meet such a legend and found him as colorful in real life as he was in the stories and books that have been written about him.

My job as an aide positively affected my family in many respects. The general's wife, June Armstrong, shepherded and mentored us in social events, teaching the proper protocol and official dining etiquette at state dinners. She'd been to Camp David when the general was flying Mrs. Eisenhower and her daughters and conveyed to us all we needed to know. We continue to remain friends with the Armstrongs.

It was during my time as the general's aide that we acquired our first dog. The children had been asking, and ten-year-old Jacky was driving us crazy with her need for a dog. We'd been given a purebred miniature black poodle. I took that little black ball of fur home, and when Jacky came home from school, I told her I had a surprise for her. We had the poodle in a little box. I will never forget her excitement. The girls were jumping up and down. Jeff was still a toddler, and not quite sure what to make of it, but he liked the puppy. Out of all the dogs we eventually adopted, this little guy was our favorite, and we named him Pretzel. I had dogs all my life, but Pretzel was one of the smartest dogs I ever had, and I grew quite attached to him.

I remember one spring vacation, when we left North Carolina for Virginia. We visited Jamestown and Williamsburg. It was a pretty day, and the girls wanted to see the revolutionary period at the Governor's Mansion. We took our little pup, Pretzel, in a basket, and let him romp in the grass. Arleen took the girls to see the exhibit, and I stayed outside with Jeff and Pretzel because Jeff was too young to enjoy it. I was watching Jeff and Pretzel playing in the grassy knolls, and I turned around to admire the mansion. On the front lawn of the mansion were two canons from the Revolutionary War. I'd only taken my eyes off my son for a few moments when I heard two ladies hollering, "Oh, don't do that. Stop! Stop!" I turned around to see my son making every effort to stuff our new puppy down the barrel of the canon. It was pretty humorous, but I scolded him and put a stop to it quickly, so as not to hurt the puppy. We also had cats while the kids were growing up, but we will always remember Pretzel as being special.

As time progressed, I began to reevaluate my life, both professionally, in the aide's position, as well as personally. Our children were getting older, and Jacky was finishing sixth grade. I began to think that a third tour, another Western Pacific tour, with its long separation from my family might not be in our best interest. I took my concerns for my family to the Lord and asked for guidance.

I still belonged to the Society of Experimental Test Pilots. That fall, when I attended the annual symposium, I met a gentleman named Jack Krings. He was the chief test pilot for McDonnell Douglas, in St. Louis, Missouri. I had toured McDonnell Douglas as a young Marine captain and was familiar with the impressive facility. McDonnell Douglas was just beginning to get into the building and design of the AV-8B Harrier. At the last symposium, I told Mr. Krings that I was thinking of getting out of the Marine Corps. He told me to send him my resume if I decided to take this step. That was all he said because the law said that was all he could say. I pondered that proposition for some time. After much prayer and discussion with Arleen, I made a decision. I began to send out resumes, beginning with Mr. Krings, and also contacted my former employer, Bob Clark, at the General Motors Company.

I was not interested in becoming an airline pilot because I enjoyed the uniqueness of flying the Harriers I'd been involved with in the Harrier program. In the fall of 1977, Jack Krings, through the McDonnell Douglas Aircraft Company, made me an offer to work for them as a test pilot. Arleen and I discussed the offer and prayed about it before we made our decision. I resigned my commission as a regular officer after eleven years in the Marine Corps to the day, December 31, 1977.

This decision was not an easy one, but I believed it was best for my family. I didn't want to become a general. As an officer becomes more senior, he or she is given desk jobs at the Pentagon. That's the nature of the beast, but I knew it wasn't for me. It wasn't just that I wanted to fly—I needed to fly; that's who I was.

I started work for McDonnell Douglas Aircraft Company in St. Louis, Missouri, as a test pilot, on January 5, 1978. I transitioned from active duty Marine Corps to a reservist and spent nineteen years in the

Reserves as a Marine officer. I spent the next twenty-six years of my professional career as a test pilot, flying fighters that were built in St. Louis during that time.

Leaving active military duty, moving into the civilian community, and working in the private sector and industry, was a big change for all of us. Prior to that time, everything we'd done, whether professionally or in our private lives, had been associated with the Marine Corps. Now, we were moving to a new and different world, and we did not know what to expect.

Arleen and I embarked on a house hunting trip to St. Louis. The children stayed back in Cherry Point with friends. We arrived in the late afternoon as it began to snow. That evening, we stayed in a hotel, and when we woke up the next morning, nearly two and a half feet of snow had blanketed the city. It was two days before we could look at any homes. Eventually, we settled on one special home and moved once again. This was probably the nicest home we'd lived in during our marriage. Although we had built a lovely home in Maryland, we were now in a community subdivision. The schools were nearby. Jacky was in seventh grade, and Kathy was starting the third grade. Jeff was the only one not yet in school.

Transitioning from a full-time military officer to the corporate world of the aerospace industry was a professional challenge. It was also a big adjustment for our family to live in the private sector. We registered the girls for school and joined Parkway Baptist Church, nearby.

Arleen and I felt like kids in a candy shop. When we lived on the base, we had a commissary and a BX. There was a Hardee's on the main road and not much else. Slim pickin's for sure. But our new home in St. Louis County was close to scores of restaurants, shopping, and businesses of all kinds. It was new and exciting, and being close to so many opportunities made us giddy, and helped ease the transition from military to civilian life.

The differences between military and civilian life soon became apparent in our new community. Now, when we attended a social function, there was a great diversity of professionals, such as doctors, businessmen, and others involved in the community, from rotary clubs and Kiwanis to hospital volunteers. We'd become so accustomed to military social life, we didn't realize our new life would bring not only diversity but a lack of community as we had known it. Although we made friends, they were distant in the respect that each person went their own way with their lives. When we went to church or a social event, people were friendly, but throughout the week we missed the camaraderie we were used to.

One day while I was busy building a deck, my daughter, chatty Kathy, came to me. Like her older sister, she loved to talk, but my mind was on the work at hand, not my motor-mouth daughter. She asked me a question which I didn't pay much attention to, and I automatically answered, "Sure, no problem." I hadn't really heard her. I was thinking about the deck, and sometimes female chatter just rattles around in a man's head without ever landing on a brain cell. I'm guilty of being that man.

Five minutes later, Arleen came around the corner of the house. "Did you say Kathy could have a rabbit?"

I groaned inside. Apparently, a friend of hers had some rabbits, and the rabbits had babies. Of course. I couldn't go back on my word to Kathy, so we built a rabbit cage, and the second of our pets showed up. We named the rabbit Chips. Now, we had Pretzel the dog and Chips the rabbit. I made a rule that the girls must take care of him.

Chips grew huge because he ate too much. He was nearly the size of a basketball. He was one of the biggest brown rabbits I'd ever seen. After about three or four months with the rabbit, the girls grew tired of providing basic care for Chips. But I believed it was important for them to learn the responsibility of having a pet and keep the commitment they made to care for him.

There were many adjustments as we eased into this new chapter of our lives, but God was with us through every step. Doors opened, doors closed, lessons were learned, and we grew closer as a family.

Jack's first photo as a McDonnell Douglas test pilot

CHAPTER 16

Black Ops with Israel

In 1979, McDonnell Douglas sent me to Israel on an intriguing assignment. I was asked to deliver a fighter aircraft to the Israeli government. However, I soon learned this would be no ordinary delivery. I departed Lambert International Airport in St. Louis at about two o'clock in the morning, and headed east. As the sun came up, I was joined by tanker aircraft for air-to-air refueling, the first of many, as I headed out over the Atlantic Ocean. Once I'd taken on enough fuel to get to the Azores Islands, in the middle of the ocean, the tankers returned to their home base.

At three o'clock in the afternoon that same day, I landed on the island, tired, and ready to get out of the jet. It had been a long day of flying, and I was looking forward to a nice dinner and a comfortable bed for some much-needed sleep. I rested the next day and did a little sightseeing around the island before embarking on another long day of flying.

Well-rested, I left the next morning bright and early. About halfway to Spain, the tankers appeared for refueling again. When I could see the coast of Spain and Africa, the tankers left and returned to their home base. As I proceeded over the Mediterranean Sea, another aircraft appeared on my radar. I broadcasted over the radio a single code word that had been given to me and received the appropriate response from the target aircraft on my radar. As we neared each other, I saw that it was an Israeli fighter aircraft, armed with missiles and machine guns, sent to escort me to the delivery point. I joined on the aircraft and flew with it to the airbase. To this day, I could not tell you the name of the air base, or where it was located.

As we were landing, it was getting dark. I saw what appeared to be two aircraft in very bad shape—something unusual for the Israeli Air Force. After we landed, I was questioned as to the maintenance of the jet I was delivering, and I answered that it was good. Immediately, they began to load the plane with ordnance to prepare it to defend their nation. I was impressed.

I was taken to a room and given some light refreshments. Then, an official instructed me to put all of my flight equipment into a box along with all my business cards and tie tack. I was told that if anyone asked me what I was doing there, I was to answer that I was a heavy equipment salesman. I understood. At no time since Israel had become a nation in 1948, was this country not surrounded by deadly enemies. I'd been sent on a black ops mission, and this was my cover.

I was escorted to a vehicle for the drive to my hotel. As we drove, I looked out the window and saw the two aircraft on land that I'd seen earlier. Now that I was closer, I could see they were plywood decoys. When we arrived at the hotel, my Israeli escorts asked me what I wanted to do the next day. I said I'd like to see their country. They agreed and informed me I would have a driver and a guide the next day for a tour.

At breakfast the next morning, I had a friendly waiter.

"I see you are an American," he said, as he poured my coffee. "What do you do?"

I had no idea whether this man was a plant, a spy, or simply what he appeared to be—a nice, friendly waiter curious about an American tourist. But I had my instructions, and I stuck by them.

"I'm a heavy equipment salesman," I answered.

He seemed satisfied. I finished my breakfast and waited to be picked up for my tour.

My entourage for the tour consisted of an Israeli soldier, a young lady, and a sixty-five-year-old driver who had survived World War II. I enjoyed the tour very much but was acutely aware of my surroundings. While my guides were present to keep me safe, and probably even out of trouble, I never lost sight of the fact that I was an American in the most hated country on the planet; a country surrounded by its enemies, and the major target of every terrorist group in existence. The very land where the Prince of Peace once walked held a round-the-clock vigil, watching for activity from her foes who wished to wipe her off the face of the map.

When it was time for me to leave Israel, an official picked me up, and we headed for the airport. We bypassed their normal security. I followed him as he stepped across the baggage check-in counter, only to be stopped by a security guard who was very upset. The two men engaged in a loud and angry conversation in Hebrew, so I didn't understand it, but in the end, I went through.

I was taken out onto the flight ramp and placed on an aircraft headed for Rome. I looked around and listened. *Nobody* was on board. I took my seat on the empty plane. Not that I watch a lot of movies, or that my imagination runs wild at any time, but an empty plane can give you a particular sense of unease. In the movies, it usually means you're about to be blown up. But I had not varied from my assignment. I'd delivered the plane as ordered with no difficulty, maintained my cover as a heavy equipment salesman, and not caused any trouble, so I had no reason to suspect anything was amiss. It was just an unusual situation. I waited for ten full minutes before the aircrew came on board. The head flight attendant approached me.

"Good morning, Mr. Jackson. Coffee?" she asked.

I told her no, and before long, we were soaring through the clouds. As the ground disappeared beneath me, it dawned on me that my passport had never been stamped. What now, I wondered?

Upon disembarking the plane in Rome, I was instructed by Israeli security to go through a particular line. When I reached the agent, he looked at my passport, stamped it and said, "Welcome to Italy." Just like that.

I spent a couple of days in Rome visiting the many beautiful sights and eating pasta, of course. I was especially fascinated by the Roman ruins and became easily lost pondering the centuries of history behind them. I came upon a tour group that had an English-speaking tour guide, so I joined the group, eager to hear the stories the guide was telling. I was caught up in her speech, when I heard a voice behind me say, "Hello, Jack." Surprised, I turned around to see a fellow Marine who'd been my catcher when I was pitching for the Navy baseball team during flight training! Talk about a small world!

I leaned in close to him, and looking around to be sure no one was paying attention, whispered, "No one is supposed to know I'm here."

He grinned and with a twinkle in his eye, whispered back to me, "Yeah, me either."

We had a great time that day in Rome, and the next day, headed home to our families.

CHAPTER 17

Testing as a Civilian

Eager to begin my new career with the McDonnell Douglas Company in St. Louis, Missouri, I was surprised to learn that the testing I had done as a military pilot was completely different from the testing I would be performing for the next twenty-six years as a civilian test pilot in industry. Being a test pilot at McDonnell Douglas required an entirely new approach. When I was hired, my background was the fleet Marine force. I believe I was hired particularly because of my AV-8A Harrier experience and completion of TPS.

I was sitting on top of the world. I'd returned home safely from the war, had a fabulous family, and now, I was getting ready to start my dream job. I thought I was pretty hot stuff, but that soon wore off when I realized there was a huge difference between being a test pilot in a civilian capacity versus military.

One of the main differences was the methodical approach to an aircraft that had not been built yet. Long before the airplane was ready to test in flight, I was involved in the designs of systems, simulation, determining how it would fly, and what the cockpit layout would be, as well as attendance at meetings.

I was impressed with and humbled by the test pilots with whom I began to work. Pat Henry was one of the most methodical test pilots I ever met. He flew a fantastic air show in the F-15. The first time I saw it, I was awestruck by the precision. When you're that good, you've arrived. But other aviators were equally impressive. John Farley, a test pilot from the United Kingdom, was the gentleman who taught me the most about being a professional test pilot. Mr. Farley was the premier Harrier test pilot from across the pond. I worked closely with Charlie Plummer, the senior test pilot for the Harrier. Charlie could read and understand systems, blueprints, and computer systems better than anyone I knew.

Bill Lowe was another gentleman with whom I worked. Nothing ever rattled Bill. The plane could be on fire, headed for the biggest city in the world, and Bill could keep his cool. I, however, was at the other end of the spectrum. I wanted to keep things moving and keep flying. I needed to slow down a bit, instead of running around with *helmet fire*, a saying in the aviation community that implies an impatient, carefree and perhaps even unprofessional attitude. Charlie and Bill reined me in. At times I felt I was being restrained. I was hot to trot and just wanted to soar through the wild blue yonder. But I had much to learn.

The longer I was there, the more I saw how important it was that each task, no matter the size, was performed correctly. Jobs were on the line and programs could be canceled if something went wrong. It was not a pretty picture. It happened to me, and it was awful.

When I started testing airplanes at McDonnell Douglas, things didn't go well for me at all. I was flying more like a Marine pilot than a test pilot. I'd just go out and fly, instead of flying with the purpose of finding out what was wrong with the aircraft. I was used to dealing with problems by finding a way to compensate and manage, rather than reporting the problems, as I was supposed to do. I was called in and told that if I couldn't figure things out, I needed to find a job elsewhere. I went to John Farley for advice. We went out for breakfast, and he began to groom me to be a professional test pilot in the civilian world. He advised me when to take a chance and when not to, how to minimize the risk, and how to make sure the jet was always in the foremost of the training. I felt like I was almost back to square one.

I became John's shadow. When we started flying the first AV-8Bs, John was there. I chased Charlie Plummer on the first flight of the AV-8B. I was just grateful to be part of the chase program. We had a problem passing 33,000 feet in altitude. The engine surged and came back. My job in the chase plane was to make sure that everything in the lead plane was clean and dry and not leaking any fuel since Charlie would be unable to see a leak from the pilot's seat.

Shortly after that, John and I went to Edwards Air Force Base in California, to do engine testing over the desert. My family stayed in Missouri. We took a team of engineers and two airplanes, both Harriers; one was a test airplane, and the other was a chase airplane. We were over the Edwards AFB big lake bed, where one of the shuttles had landed early on. It's a large, prehistoric dry lake bed about seven miles long and five miles wide. The engine testing involved shutting it down and defining the envelope. To define an envelope means to test a plane to see where the limits of safety are so that a pilot knows not to go beyond a certain parameter. To push the envelope is akin to going to the edge of a cliff and sticking one foot over. As long as you stay on the cliff, you won't fall. When we test an aircraft to define the envelope, we see how fast it can go, how high it can go, etcetera, and still stay within the limits of safety. We see where the parameters are so a pilot knows not to go beyond that point.

Generally, two flights went out a day, weather permitting. John would fly the test airplane one time, while I would chase, then we would reverse it. We'd have lunch and talk. In the evening, we'd have dinner together and discuss the day's events. I watched him carefully. John was immensely important to my career in aviation, especially as a test pilot. We did a lot of testing. Sometimes the engines would start, and sometimes they wouldn't. We would push the envelope. John would rein me in when I got too aggressive. Charlie and Bill were in Maryland at the time, doing other testing. I owe a debt of gratitude to Charlie and Bill for their valuable help in my early career, but even more so to John.

As my test pilot career progressed at McDonnell Douglas, I realized that my philosophy needed to change. I began to work with the government test pilots, many of whom were friends of mine from the Marine Corps. I learned that a civilian test pilot is the umpire of the testing community in aerospace. You call it like you see it. If the company is right, then the company is right, and if the customer is right, then the customer is right. You do the right thing, and sometimes you make the company, that is, your bosses, angry. Sometimes you have to tell the customer that that's the way it is, and if you want to make a change, you have to pay for it. You will almost always be unpopular with somebody. Later in life, as I entered politics, that was doubly reinforced. Such is life, whether in the workplace or in public service. As long as Arleen wasn't angry with me, I could deal with it!

Today, the military has become more involved with the testing. I don't agree with that idea. I believe the contractor should be held accountable for the airplane he builds, and when the customer starts flying and testing early on, the company has no way of correcting any deficiency. This philosophy has developed over the years, resulting in the cost of manufacturing a weapons system escalating to the point of being unbearable for the taxpayer. When I was an elected official, I realized that there's a time when the government must allow the private sector to do what it does best, and the government must stay out of it. The government should only become involved if someone is not playing by the rules, in which case, punishment must be swift and severe.

However, if the private sector is doing the right thing, then the government should stay out of their business and let them do it. When the project is finished, the company can present it for evaluation. But the system currently in place is extremely and unnecessarily expensive.

We performed three types of pilot testing at McDonnell Douglas: production, engineering, and experimental.

The production test pilot position requires flying production airplanes as they come off the assembly line to ensure everything is working, and getting it to the customer to fly it and take it to the fleet.

The second phase, the engineering test pilot, takes an aircraft that has been approved as a product but may need a new computer installed, requiring testing and new software, for example. Then, only that part requires evaluation, since the airplane has already been proven.

The experimental test flying was the third and most demanding phase. This consisted of taking the airplane up for the first time and expanding the envelope. I had to check structures, flutter, flying qualities, and weapons systems. We did *a lot* of flying. In the experimental test flying, the test pilot would put the airplane into a downward spin. This was an extremely important program that required expertise in several areas. I was privileged to fly some first flights on variations of airplanes. The first was the AV-8C, a variation of the A model with some additional modifications to it. I flew the first flight on the night attack version of the Harrier, and radar version of the AV-8B. It had the same name, but came with big changes.

I also had the privilege of flying the F-15 and engaging in work with that. It was well developed, so my

testing in that particular aircraft was just at the engineering test pilot level. I did a lot of production flying
in it. I also received experimental work in the F-18 because it was starting at the same time as the Harrier.

To keep our family together, we moved back to
Patuxent River, Maryland, for that year, but we returned to St. Louis and built a home because Arleen
and I felt it was important that our family have roots,
and the St. Louis area was a great place to work and
raise a family. Thankfully, this was the last move we
would make with our children. St. Louis was home.
Period.

The McDonnell Douglas Corporation was one
of the finest companies for which I had the privilege
of working. They were professional in all aspects.
Working for people like Sandy McDonnell, the CEO,
and Bill Ross, the president of the company, taught
me how a senior executive should act. The lessons I
learned during those years carried me through the
rest of my life.

Another individual, John Capalupo, made a strong
impression on me. He and Sandy McDonnell ruled
in much the same way. They had an iron hand on the
company. But covering that iron hand was a silk glove.
They understood that their employees were the most
important resource in the company. I was impressed
with their philosophy. If more employers treated their
employees with dignity and respect and realized that
each employee is valuable to the company's success,
the many benefits realized in every aspect of the business would be evident to both employer and employee.

The longer I worked at McDonnell Douglas, the
more involved and expanded the testing became.
Twenty-six years is a long time to test. The job was
never dull. Flying is exciting, and pushing the limits
of an aircraft, to see what it can and cannot do is exhilarating.

One of the highlights of my first flight was the flutter testing in an F-18 jet. This is where I flew the aircraft low, at five or six thousand feet, at a high rate of speed. I turned on a computer which had been installed only in the test airplane, and it would move the flight controls at various speeds and rates to see if they were going to continue the flutter and get worse. The flutter is to determine if the flight control service starts to move in a certain way. If it continues, it will probably self-destruct. This is quite dangerous, of course.

A hair-raising incident occurred when I was flying an F-18 on a flutter test. On this particular test flight, we were on the coast of Maryland, over the Atlantic Ocean. I was at about five thousand feet, and going extremely fast. It was a clear, pretty day, which was important, as bad weather can affect or cancel a test. I turned on the flutter computer to start the test point. We were in excess of five hundred fifty knots and had a safety chase plane with us. Suddenly, in the middle of the test, all of the warning lights came on. That is never a good sign. The aircraft pitched violently nose up, bells began ringing, and then suddenly, everything went silent. I promptly pulled the throttles to idle, thinking I would have to eject, and slowed the airplane as quickly as I could. All the radios were dead, so communications were non-existent. I managed to get the airplane leveled off to fly, but the plane was very sluggish. I was still unable to talk to anyone. I could feel the airplane accelerate, and when I pulled it back, it would decelerate. I thought I was pretty far out to sea, and as long as it was still running, I slowed it down. I had airspeed and altitude on the standby gauges, but everything else was dead. As I turned back to the west, I saw the mouth of the Chesapeake Bay, and I knew the Patuxent River was up the bay, so I found the mouth of the bay and headed back to home base.

As I approached the bay, the airport came into view. I made a circle overhead, rocked the wings a little bit, and the control tower cleared the airspace out for me when they finally saw me. When the tower sees a plane rocking its wings, it signifies that the pilot has no communications working and so the tower will clear the runway and give the pilot a green light when it's safe to land.

My next concern was the landing gear. I had no indication when I put it down that it had, in fact, gone down. I could only assume, so I used the emergency extension as well and blew the gear down just to double check it. Still no indication. I came in and made the landing. Even though I had little breaking, I did get the plane stopped, and taxied clear the runway—but I had no nose wheel steering. I shut the plane down where I stopped and managed to open the canopy and get out. The emergency crews were already there, of course. I was breathing hard and could feel my heartbeat pounding in my chest. I had no idea how or why this test had gone so dangerously wrong, but I was grateful to be on solid ground.

I explained what happened. I never saw the chase plane. He lost sight of me when I pitched up, and because I couldn't talk to him, he returned, thinking I had crashed.

Once my heart rate and blood pressure returned to normal, I had to admit it was quite a ride—but all is not lost in this type of adventure. We examined the jet to discover what had happened. On the right side of the panel, near the nose, just forward of the cockpit, was an electric wire bundle, about two inches in diameter. The panel that covered it had a 3/4-inch screw holding the panel onto the side of the airplane. An electric wire cable ran along the side of this panel. Someone had replaced the 3/4-inch screw which held the panel on with a screw that was two inches long.

This screw had been pushed into the electric wiring bundle and shorted out everything in the airplane. Something so small and seemingly insignificant nearly cost McDonnell Douglas a plane and could have cost me my life. I got the airplane back safely. Simply stated, this heart-stopping event was all because some mechanic put in the wrong screw!

This dangerous incident taught us that you cannot have a wire bundle like this next to a panel where everything can be shorted out because the F-18 is a combat airplane. Had the plane taken a bullet there, it would've had the same effect. To remedy the problem, we split the wires up, moved them around, and changed the size of the panel.

As harrowing as the F-18 incident was, it paled in comparison to a test flight I did on a cold day in November 1979. I took off from St. Louis with my chase plane to test the engine performance on a prototype aircraft. Only two of these prototype planes had been built, and I was testing one of them. We were flying southeast of the Lake of the Ozarks over a heavily wooded area. All I could see below me for miles was the forest.

The test maneuver started out at thirty-nine thousand feet, and two hundred knots. I rolled the aircraft into a left-hand turn, with the throttle at idle. Then I slammed into full throttle. The engine gave a loud backfire, or surge. I responded to this by immediately pulling the throttle to idle, to see if the backfiring would stop. It did not.

Following procedure, I shut off the engine, so as not to damage it or cause a fire. At this point, I could do nothing but roll the wings level and start gliding down to an altitude of twenty thousand feet. The engine produced a lot of clanging and banging noises. At twenty thousand feet, I commenced to try an air start.

The result of the first attempt was that the engine did
not start. I waited for another five thousand feet, until
I was at 15,000 feet, and attempted another air start.
This also failed.

The pilot in my chase plane reported to me that
gas was leaking out of the exhaust, but it did not seem
to be igniting. I tried this process several more times,
and during these attempts, I raised the visor on my
helmet to make sure I could see the engine gauges
properly. By the time I'd fallen to two thousand feet,
it was apparent to me the engine was not going to
re-start, and I was going to have to eject because the
plane was going down.

As I started the ejection process, I looked up, and
there seemed to be two million trees all around, and
just ahead, one little town. Just my luck. One small
town surrounded by a massive forest. A very bad situation had just gotten worse. My plane was headed
straight for that little town.

I turned the airplane away from the town, and assumed the ejection position, which is back straight
against the seat, head against the seat rest, and elbows
in, to not injure my back, neck, or head. The ejection
handle is about the size of a horseshoe, and it sits between your knees. When the handle is pulled, the pilot
is supposed to be ejected out of the airplane in 1.4 seconds. I pulled the handle, and it felt like three years
went by, because that seat did not fire. I continued to
lose altitude. When I looked down from my straight up-
right position to see what was wrong with the ejection
handle, the seat fired. On most modern-day aircraft,
during ejection, the canopy departs the airplane completely, and then the ejection takes place. Because this
was a prototype airplane, one out of only two built, the
canopy had an explosive charge which blew the glass
and shrapnel out, instead of having the canopy leave
the aircraft. However, at this point, because I had my

visor up and was looking down to see why my seat had not ejected when it was supposed to, all that shrapnel and glass flew into my face and eyes. I left the aircraft in the position of someone reaching down to tie their shoes, which is totally wrong. As I was thrust from the plane, I felt the parachute open, but when I looked up, I couldn't see anything. Then it dawned on me—my helmet, which had black leather inside, had slipped down over my eyes. When I pulled it up out of my eyes so I could see, I couldn't breathe. I couldn't figure out why I couldn't breathe until I remembered my oxygen mask was now over my face again, but the actual oxygen had crashed with the airplane. So I unhooked my oxygen mask and I could breathe again. My face really hurt, and when I touched it, there was blood on my flight glove. I knew then I was hurt.

The first thing I was taught to do after ejection is to look up and see if the parachute canopy is okay, and mine was. I looked beneath me to see where I was going to come down, and there were trees everywhere, except off to my left, where I could see an open field. I knew I didn't want to come down in the trees, so I pulled on the riser to guide myself to the left to come down in the field. But when I reached up and pulled the left riser, instead of going in the direction I was trying to steer, the chute started to collapse. I took my hands off the riser and yelled at the parachute, "Take me where you want—just don't collapse!" Since then, I've often thought that's the way God works with me. It isn't until my life parachute starts to collapse that I tell Him to take me where He wants—just don't collapse.

I came crashing down through the tree limbs with my legs crossed and arms folded so I would not get punctured by a tree limb. My parachute caught on a low-hanging branch, leaving me dangling about three feet off the ground. I unhooked my parachute and dropped to the ground. My chase plane made a low pass, and I waved to him, indicating I was okay.

The aircraft I was testing went down in the forest with a tremendous crash and exploded into a huge and very hot fireball. The wing was not made of metal and burned even hotter. I was just grateful that it didn't go down into that little town. No life was lost.

Free of the parachute, I found myself standing in the middle of a pasture full of cattle. I was wearing a red flight suit and cattle were running everywhere. I thought with the day I was having, there was bound to be one angry bull in this field, and he would, of course, charge at my red flight suit. But because my wingman had made a low pass, the cattle were frightened and scattered away from me.

I started to walk towards the road. Two men came running toward me, forming a V as they ran, one on my left, one on my right. The man on the left, whom I never met or saw again, got within fifty yards of me. I believe he meant to say "Are you hurt?" But instead, at the top of his lungs, he hollered, "Are you dead?"

I hollered back, "No."

He answered "Okay," and turned and left. I guess his breakfast was getting cold.

The guy on my right, whose name I found out later was Floyd, ran up to me, out of breath. I told him, "I gotta get to a phone!"

Floyd answered, "You gotta get to a doctor."

"Phone first."

My plane had gone down at about 8:40 a.m. Floyd took me to his house in his truck. Not much was said until we got there, but then he turned to me and said, "Young man, you've had a rough morning. Do you want a beer?"

"No, thanks."

If a pilot is involved in this kind of an accident, he is thoroughly tested to see what foods were eaten, what beverages were drunk, how many hours he slept, and anything else that can be tested to see if there is any physiological explanation for the accident. If Boeing had found alcohol in my blood, I'd have been strung up by my thumbs. I understood the man meant well, though. Plenty of people turn to alcohol to steady their nerves, calm them down, or make them feel better, especially after something as traumatic as a plane accident. But for a pilot to do so would mean the end of his flying career.

When we got to his house, Floyd's wife came out to the truck, accompanied by three young women. Floyd, being a friendly sort of gentleman, and not wanting to be inhospitable, began to introduce me to all of them.

"This is my wife. This is my oldest daughter. This is my youngest daughter. And, this is my wife's younger sister. She's visiting us from Texas."

Floyd's wife shot him an exasperated look, and in a very stern voice, said, "Floyd, can't you see he's hurt? We gotta get him inside!"

They took me into the house where I made a phone call to work to let them know I was alive and tell them what had happened. Floyd's wife took a washcloth and began to gently clean my face. As she wiped off the blood, she said, "You gotta get to a doctor."

The company told me when I talked to them on the phone, to get to the nearest airport, that they were sending an airplane to pick me up. Having taken off from St. Louis, I was a long way from home.

Floyd drove me to Lee C. Fine Airport. When I got there, the local sheriff met us and asked what he could do for me.

I said, "I'm going to the back room to lie down."

Not one to miss the obvious, he said, "Your eyes are swollen shut."

I could tell not much got by the sheriff there, and said, "I know. The press is going to come. Keep them away from me."

The airport manager was a big guy, around six foot four, and easily two hundred thirty pounds. He motioned to me and said, "Come on in the back room and lie down on the couch." He didn't have to tell me twice.

Shortly after that, the press from two different television channels arrived. I could hear the commotion from where I was resting. They said they'd heard the pilot of the airplane that crashed was here and demanded to see me.

The sheriff, no fan of reporters, said, "No, he's not here."

They snickered and answered, "Come on, we know he's here."

The manager slammed the door to the room where I was lying on the couch, and I heard him yell in a gruff voice, "The sheriff told you, he's not here. Now get out of my airport."

They left.

The company plane picked me up a couple of hours later, and I had eye surgery the next day.

There was only one private room available at the hospital, and Boeing wanted me to have it. Unfortunately, it was in the maternity ward. The head nurse assigned to me was a stately and powerful woman. That night I asked her, "Could you wash my hair before surgery tomorrow?" The only way this could happen was for me to lean backward over a sink so the soap wouldn't get in my eyes. I was wearing a hospital gown, and as she was washing my hair, I didn't realize that my hospital gown had ridden up and I was providing quite a show. Then I heard three or four women giggling. I didn't see these ladies in the maternity ward, but I heard the head nurse say, "Get outta here, girls. You've seen that before. That's how you got here!" I never said a word, but I do know what it feels like to die a thousand deaths.

The eye surgery itself was brutal. The surgeon, Dr. Harry Eggleston, told me I had two options. The first was for him to numb everything around my eyeballs with tiny needles and then perform the surgery. But, there was a small risk of loss of vision with this procedure. I reminded Dr. Eggleston that I was a pilot and made my living with my eyes. I asked what plan B was?

Plan B was that he wouldn't numb my eyes. I would have to hold very still while he picked out the glass and shrapnel. Dr. Eggleston told me I wouldn't feel any pain from the eyeball itself because it had no nerve endings. I chose Plan B.

When they rolled me into the operating room, the nurses began to tie down my hands to the bed. They fastened a large strap across my chest and wedged my head so it could not move.

"You don't have to do this, I can hold still."

One of the nurses replied, "We don't care how strong a person you think you are. When someone comes at your eyes, your natural reflex is to put your hand up, and move your head."

I hadn't thought of that. They took small wedges and propped my eyes open so I couldn't blink. When the doctor got there, they ran water on my eyeball, as he picked out the shrapnel. I felt little or no pain, but I thought this must be similar to Chinese torture with all that water.

The doctor removed every piece of shrapnel except one in my right eye, which fortunately left no effect on my vision. The end result of the surgery was that my vision returned to 20/15, and to this day, I do not wear glasses. Dr. Harry Eggleston saved my vision. Whenever I see Dr. Eggleston, I never say hello—I do, however, always say, "It's very good to see you, doctor."

Arleen was in Maryland with the children and didn't learn of my ejection and injuries until a friend of ours, John Junek, a captain in the Navy, called her and said, "Jack has ejected. He was hurt. He had surgery, but he's okay." I had never gotten a chance to call her because the company and their lawyers had questioned me as to what happened for hours. Two days later I was flown in a private jet to Maryland where Arleen and the kids met me, and I spent two months recuperating. I'm happy to report that in spite of my injuries, I'm still the handsome devil I always was.

The investigation into the accident took eleven months. It was in the company's best interest to determine the crash was due to pilot error, and they tried to prove I was to blame. But it wasn't my error, and the investigators could find no evidence to support such a finding.

For me, losing that airplane was like parting with a good friend, almost like a death. I was mad at the plane, and I was mad at myself. During the investigation, I'd wake up at 2 a.m., wondering if I'd caused this accident. Was it pilot error? Was there something I did wrong or could've done differently? Jobs were on the line. Somebody somewhere had made a mistake. The pressure robbed me of sleep.

Two years later, we found out what caused the accident when we were doing some testing at Edwards Air Force Base. The ignition system had failed, and no spark was lighting the gas.

It wasn't until we took the second plane to Edwards Air Force Base for testing that we discovered the problem. The original system failed again, and the engine did not start. The plane was originally built with a series of nine electrical relays connecting the start button to the engine. If only one of those relays failed to spark, the engine would not start. We then ran a separate wire directly from the start button to the engine, bypassing the original system, and the problem was solved. The new backup system is presently in the Harrier jets.

While the excitement, danger, and prestige surrounding the career of a test pilot made me feel on top of the world, I still wanted my parents to be proud of me. We took a brief break to visit my family in Indiana where I proudly showed my parents my business card. I stood back, waiting to hear how proud they were to raise a son who was now a professional in a field that few people ever enter.

"Jack Jackson Test Pilot," my dad read as he turned my card over in his hand. "So you're a test pilot? That takes nerves of steel, iron for blood, and dirt for brains!"

My mom shook her head and added, "I raised you better than that."

As the years progressed, I moved up to Chief Pilot for Production Test and was responsible for the production of all the airplanes.

At the same time, I had been given command of a troubled Marine squadron in Memphis, Tennessee, as a reserve lieutenant colonel. The squadron was struggling because of difficulty with the more senior officers. It was like working two full-time jobs and made for a great deal of stress. Once again, Arleen was left to run our home and family with little help from me. It was by the grace of God that we got through such a crazy-busy schedule.

In addition, I was still doing Harrier testing. I was handed a program called a T-45 Goshawk. It was difficult getting this airplane into the fleet. I won't belabor all the issues we had with it but will mention a few. Response time with the throttle was slow. There were problems with its stall characteristics. This little T-45 Goshawk is a trainer airplane, which I'm proud to say is in service today in the Navy's fleet in the advanced trainer. It was a derivative of the British Hawk. What we'd attempted to do was take a land-based trainer airplane and make it a carrier-based trainer airplane. That was an enormous transition with stalls, transitions, carrier landings, and structural integrity.

I never worked as hard as I worked in 1989, being the CO of a reserve squadron with issues, taking on a T-45, and still working with the Harrier program to keep it moving. It was an extremely busy and very tough year. But God is always good. Isaiah tells us, "Thou wilt keep him in perfect peace whose mind is staid on Thee because he trusteth in thee." (Isa. 26:3). I don't think I could have gotten through such rigorous demands without the peace of God to keep me sane.

Other areas I worked in during my test pilot career I found were just as intriguing. I remember the first time I flew using night vision goggles. It was like strapping a pair of binoculars on my head and turning out all the lights, so I was in total darkness, and then flying around. The first time I flew with them, the medical doctors told us that these goggles weighed about four pounds. They warned us not to eject while wearing them because they would break our necks. Nice to know. I practiced extensively removing those goggles before I flew with them. Today's goggles are only three-quarters of a pound, and they see much better in the night. Today's military is light years ahead in every aspect of preparedness since I served in Vietnam. But it's always exciting to be on the vanguard of progress, especially when you're working to make your country safer by improving the equipment and technology for future generations.

It was quite an experience learning how to fly using the night goggles and adjusting to the lighting. There were some things I could see, but other things just blended into everything else. The cockpit lighting had to be changed, but the night vision goggles and the night attack Harrier that we built with the flare in the nose changed warfare as we knew it, by providing the ability to see at night almost as clearly as one would see in the daytime.

We also put radar in the nose of a Harrier. We called it the Harrier 2 Plus and tested the radar and flying qualities. The difference between radar and a flare is that the flare senses heat, and you can tell whether it's white-hot or black-hot. Radar senses an object.

Some of these weapons systems are fighting the war on terrorism today. I am honored to have been a part of it, to feel the thrill of accomplishment in knowing that I helped to usher in a new era of weaponry as today's military defends our country against those who seek to destroy it. It was an exciting time to be a test pilot.

Jack as chief test pilot for the Harrier at Boeing.

CHAPTER 18

Cloak and Dagger Intrigue in Russia

The year 1995 marked one of the most exciting highlights of my aviation career. I was assigned to go to Russia to fly two Russian fighters, the SUU27, and the YAK38. This opportunity had its origins three years earlier, in 1992, but it wasn't until 1995, that I actually left for Russia to fly the airplanes.

In 1992, I first met the chief pilot for Sukhoi, in Oklahoma City, and again in St. Louis. The Russians at that time had brought two SUU27s to the United States to display them and to see if any of their aerospace technology would fit into the Western world.

I was briefed by two agencies as to what I should expect in my meeting with the chief pilot for Sukhoi and learned a few Russian words and phrases in preparation for my trip. I was also warned to watch for the KGB.

The chief pilot and I talked about airplanes. There's an unwritten code of honor among professional test pilots. If two test pilots are talking to one another and they work for competitors, for example, the Boeing Company and Lockheed Martin, it has been my experience that one test pilot would never lie to the other test pilot. I was always careful to never ask another test pilot a question that would make him feel compelled to lie. In my conversations with the Russian pilot, only generalities about the airplanes were discussed, but never anything specific, as that could risk national security.

At dinner one evening, we were talking about our families. I told him about my family, my children and by now, grandchildren, and he told me about his. He had two children. One was a captain in the Russian Air Force, but he was not a pilot. He was an engineer who worked on aircraft engines. He also had a daughter that was much younger. It was fortunate for me that I remembered the details of this small talk, as I would need it in the future; but I didn't know it at that time.

In 1995, we finally got approval, visas, and passports for me and another engineer, Paul Reger, to travel to Russia to fly these two airplanes. Paul and I left St. Louis, flew into Paris, and then into Moscow. We arrived at the Moscow airport, and after being briefed, we were instructed not to get into any taxis. There were specific people we were told to look for with specific identification. The Chechnyan War was going on at that time. Every foreseeable security measure was taken as Paul and I ventured into the unknown. The one thing we did know, was that the KGB was everywhere. Safety was a prime concern.

When we landed in Moscow, there was no mistaking that we'd left the clean, crisp ambiance of the United States and Western Europe. The airport in Moscow was dirty and in serious need of basic maintenance. Several light bulbs were either out or missing altogether and the corridors of the airport were dark and ominous. It was almost midnight. We only had carry-on luggage. As Paul and I exited the airplane and walked through the gate, we spotted the man who was our point of contact. He showed us a photo ID and gave us a code word. We used the appropriate signals to identify ourselves and to identify him. He took us to a car and drove us to the hotel compound, situated in a guarded and gated area with a high wall. I was encouraged to see we would be staying at a Sheraton Hotel, and when we entered, the lobby was nice. Our point of contact got us registered at the front desk. It was a Sunday night, and he told us to take Monday off to allow our bodies time to recover from jetlag. He told us that our driver and interpreter would pick us up in the lobby on Tuesday at nine o'clock in the morning. We said goodnight, and Paul and I went upstairs.

Our rooms were not nearly as nice as the lobby. They were, at least, clean, and we had our own bathrooms, which, in this part of the world, was as luxurious as one could hope. The furnishings were somewhat sparse, not what one would expect in a Sheraton Hotel in other parts of the world, yet this hotel was one of the nicer hotels in the Moscow area.

I slept well that night, and the next morning when we got up, we thought we'd take a quick tour of the area since we had the day off. We didn't know much about our location, but we talked to the concierge. The front desk staff warned us to watch out for the gypsies. I only saw a couple of seven or eight-year-old boys kicking a soccer ball around. When we smiled and waved, they smiled and waved back. Children are children, regardless of where they live in the world. They are a precious asset.

Paul and I went to Red Square. I was surprised at how large it was. As a young man, I had watched the Russian military march across the Red Square on their May Day Celebration, showing their massive troops and arms displays. We looked at the tombs of some of their leaders outside the wall of the Kremlin. There was a place they called the Gym. It was Russia's version of a large mall. They had mostly American or European items in it. The shelves were poorly stocked back then, but I would imagine that's changed since my visit in 1995.

We toured the inside of the Kremlin. There was a place inside called the Armory, which, when we bought the tickets to go in, I assumed would be a display of weapons, since that's what the word means in the United States. However, it was an enormous three-story building which housed all of the crown jewels from Russian history. I was amazed at the vast wealth of the past monarchies, even in Stalin's reign. The crowns, gold cups, and carriages were stunning and impressive. I believe that if Russia had cashed in some of these assets, they could have been a more powerful nation. I learned while I was there, that because of their national economy, Russia was considered a third world country.

We saw some of their small churches. At the time, the Russian Christians were starting to put the crosses back on top of their churches which had been torn down during the previous Communist reign. I reflected on how, in the United States, any house of worship, regardless of the faith taught within its walls, is free to place their symbols in plain sight, and how easy it is to take that freedom for granted. Russian Christians risked their lives for merely attending church, or even owning a portion of a Bible. Children of Russian Christians were ripped from their homes and sent to re-education camps. Some had been forced to kill their own parents or watch as the Communists slaughtered family members for their faith. It was especially disconcerting to learn how horribly Christians in Communist countries were persecuted for their faith when in America, lukewarm churchgoers believe they're doing God a favor when they show up to warm a pew a few times a year. It encouraged my heart to see crosses beginning to sprout up on Russian churches.

Late that afternoon, Paul and I decided to get some exercise, since our hotel had an exercise room. While I was doing push-ups, my shoulder popped out of joint, and I collapsed in a heap. The pain was so great, it was all I could do just to keep from passing out. Among the other hotel guests that were also exercising, was a lady. This lady saw me get up on my knees to try to get my senses back. She told me I had dislocated my shoulder. I pushed it, but the pain was so intense, I almost went down again. She motioned to her husband, who, thankfully, was a physician. He came to me and readjusted my shoulder. Paul told me I needed to ice it. I went back to the room, but there were no ice cubes; only a small refrigerator with two bottles of water in it. I wrapped a towel around the bottles of water and put those on my shoulder. I managed to eat a little dinner.

The next day, my shoulder was moveable and functional, but decidedly black and blue. All I could think of was that I had come all the way to Russia and would not be able to fly because of my shoulder. I worked most of the day trying to keep it loose and not let it tighten up on me.

The next morning at 9 a.m., Paul and I went to the hotel lobby where a young lady of about eighteen, and a man around thirty-five years of age were waiting for us. The man was our driver. The young lady informed me that she was our interpreter for the day, and she was just learning English. She asked us if it was okay to be our interpreter. I introduced her to Paul. She told us that our driver did not speak English, but he was very knowledgeable and would be able to get us out of the city and near the test center.

Then she said something that startled me. "You knew my father."

I replied, "Really?"

She mentioned his name, which I recognized as the Russian pilot whom I had met three years earlier. I asked, "How is your father doing?"

She told me, "He was killed six months ago."

He had been killed testing an airplane. I told her I was sorry to hear that and hoped she and her mother were doing all right. Then I pressed her further, to see if this girl was true, or if she was a KGB plant. I asked her, "You have a brother who is a captain in the Russian Air Force. What airplanes does he fly?"

She said, "I have a brother, but he does not fly airplanes. He is an engineer designing engines."

I knew this was the correct answer because I had remembered the conversation I'd had with her father three years ago. I suppose she could have been a plant, but I didn't think she was.

We left the hotel compound. As we drove through the city, I noticed a huge crowd in front of a building in downtown Moscow. I asked her, "What's going on?"

"A McDonald's restaurant has opened several weeks ago, but you must wait in line for about three hours just to get a hamburger."

I found that amazing, but then, I would not wait three seconds to get a hamburger from McDonald's, let alone three hours. Moreover, I did not live in a country that experienced food shortages.

We drove about an hour before we were out of Moscow. The roads went from four-lane paved to two-lane paved. I noticed gasoline trucks parked alongside the road and asked what they were there for. Our interpreter informed me that was where you buy gas for your car. People would stop by the truck, it would fill up their car, and they would pay the truck driver and go on their way.

The drive took us from paved roads to poorly paved roads to gravel roads. After another hour, we came to an entrance surrounded by an imposing brick wall with an iron gate that must have been three stories high. The car pulled up to the gate and stopped. A woman came out and took all of our passports and identification, and disappeared. Behind the giant fence, armed guards patrolled everywhere because Russia was at war with Chechnya. During all my travels abroad, I never felt more uncomfortable than I did at this time. If this was a trap and this woman had stolen our passports, we could be left stranded, alone with no identification, miles from Moscow.

Finally, the woman returned with our passports and identification. The gates opened and we drove about a half mile on a gravel road through a wooded area. We came out of the woods onto one of the largest testing facilities I'd ever seen. Airplanes were everywhere, most of them parked in the middle of a long runway. We had requested permission in advance to take pictures and videos in order to determine if any of the Russian aerospace industry would fit in with ours. Surprisingly, our request was granted.

We drove to their headquarters and met with the dignitaries to discuss the planes we would fly and our evaluations. I made up a test card for evaluation of both airplanes I was to fly. The people we dealt with were genuine and hospitable, and I relaxed somewhat. I never felt threatened, although I was cautious at all times and guarded in what I said.

The furniture in the building was old. There was a threadbare green couch with a matching chair and two wooden kitchen chairs that looked like they'd been used as chew toys by a Rottweiler. We were offered some store-bought cookies. They were ordinary wafer cookies, but the Russians considered them a delicacy. Our lunch was potatoes and beef, with bottled water to drink. Four restrooms were available. Three were disgusting and out of service.

They required all pilots to have a physical to fly their airplanes. I'd seen this done with the dignitaries I've flown, so it came as no surprise. A physician would be present to check the heart and blood pressure just before a ride, and then I would sign a waiver. I expected the same or similar here. I introduced myself to the nurse, who could have passed for Dolly Parton's twin. I thought, Deodorant, don't fail me now!

In broken English, she asked me how I felt. I told her I felt fine. She replied, "Okay." We both signed the waiver, and I went out to fly. Good thing I was in excellent health, with the exception of my shoulder! We were suited up with flight equipment which had some nice features.

The first airplane I flew was the YAK38, Russia's answer to the Harrier. As we got into the brief, I told them what I wanted to do, and how I would like to evaluate the YAK. Their concept had three engines. This concept was totally different from what I was used to on the Harrier AV-8B Jump Jet, which only had one engine. On the YAK, two of the engines were mounted perpendicular to the ground, and one was mounted horizontally to the ground like a conventional engine in an aircraft. The Russians had lowered the nozzles on the larger horizontal engine, then the two engines that sat perpendicular to the ground had doors that opened, and they were the front lift engines providing the hover post. I was impressed they had manufactured a fuel control that controlled three different engines with one throttle. That was nice. However, I did not like the three-engine concept. It took a long time to get the engine started before I could begin to hover the aircraft. In addition, the aircraft had to hover at one hundred fifty feet above the ground, or at least, that's what they told me. The Harrier hovered at around fifty feet above the ground. The engines on the YAK38 burned extremely hot, so they had to use a special metal. It would even damage concrete if left on it too long, so when I returned from my flight and made the vertical landing, they shut the engines down and got the nozzles aft very quickly.

I was flying with a gentleman named Igor. We made the takeoff and went out into the area. I saw how fast it went, and how it turned. In an airplane that hovers, the flight controls are supposed to be extremely light and easily moved. This airplane felt too heavy, and I didn't think it was right. Igor did not know who I was, and he spoke broken English. He probably didn't know how good a pilot I was and likely didn't trust me, so I asked him, "Igor, are you on the flight controls?"

He said, "No, no, no."

But it was still heavy. I said to him, "Igor, if you are on the flight controls, I am going to ask for my money back."

All of a sudden, the flight controls got very light. I chuckled at that because it's the same the world over. Customer satisfaction and the money you pay are important. We returned, and I landed the airplane and went through the debrief. I was pleased with it.

Two days later, we flew the SUU27, which I was impressed with because it was a large airplane. It had what I call a combination of our F-14 Tomcat technology and our F-15 Eagle technology. It was one of the finest blends of an aerodynamic shape and a flyby wire flight control system I had ever flown. It did the Cobra maneuver, which allowed the airplane to go straight up and then slide back down and pitch forward with full power, an impressive maneuver.

The Russians were lacking in other areas, though, such as human factors and how they put the cockpits together. All in all, I was impressed with both the airplanes.

The Russian government, like all Communist governments, underestimated the intelligence of its own people. Rather than allow the people to use their own brains and think for themselves, they used brute force by imposing their views on the people in every area of life—a *my way or the highway* mentality. If they allowed more free enterprise, then the resources and the intelligence they already had would render them a power to be reckoned with. But because of the form of government they're under, the people were suppressed, and with that type of suppression, creativity and progress are hindered.

I had been warned about the KGB, and it wasn't long before their presence became known.

During the entire time I was at the testing facility, there was a man who followed me around everywhere. Dressed in a light blue windbreaker, blue jeans, and tennis shoes, his appearance was not too sinister, but he shadowed me at all times. Of course, there was quite an entourage, so we had plenty of company everywhere we went, as a matter of their own security.

When we were on the flight ramp, there was one particular hangar overlooking the various airplanes, which I was told not to go near. Now, for me, that was like throwing a bone to a dog!

One day, when things were slow, and they were preparing the airplane, I was out on the flight ramp. I walked over and opened the door to this hangar and looked inside. There sat Russia's newest version of a vertical takeoff and land aircraft—the plane we'd not been allowed to see. I stood there a minute, before the gentleman in the blue windbreaker caught up to me and told me I should not be there. I told him I was confused and I was sorry.

He said, "You are not supposed to be here. Come with me."

I asked him, "What do you do?"

He became gruff with his answer. "I work as a night watchman in a bank."

Now, I hadn't smarted off to anybody in a while, so I was overdue. If this guy was a night watchman in a bank, then I was a florist. Unable to keep my mouth shut or engage in small talk, I asked him, "Is that the First National Bank of the KGB?"

He turned to me, and we stared at each other maybe thirty yards from the hangar and thirty yards from the airplane. We were like two cats in a staring contest. He stared at me, and I stared back at him. I was not going to be stared down if it took all day and my eyeballs dried out.

He finally spoke. "Mr. Jackson, we know you are the most experienced VSTOL pilot in the world. We know you served in Vietnam. We know the number of medals you have. We know you have been a test pilot. We know the names of your children and your grandchildren."

I continued staring at him, refusing to be intimidated, and answered, "I guess the KGB is alive and well."

Without another word, we turned and walked away, shoulder to shoulder. The shiver that shot down my spine was known only to me. Like the commercial says, "Never let them see you sweat." It was a wake-up call for me that even in 1995, things had not really changed. I believe that is still true today. I believe the Russians are continuing to work their way back to what they were before the Cold War.

Their flight ramps were covered with grass and dirt. They weren't clean, like the ramps on our military bases. I had no idea how the airplanes were maintained. I noticed a few leaks, but nothing serious. In the run of the videos, they got a wheel truck stuck under the wheel. A guy went over to the car and just beat it out with a tire tool. The tire tool got caught, and it left a gash in the tire, but they left it there; they didn't care. Their standards were a little less than ours, but I never doubted their professionalism in the least. Because of the restrictions and secrecy, no one person was fully aware of what was totally going on, except at the higher levels of the government.

When Paul and I went back that day, having flown the airplanes, they looked at our data. They told us we were welcome to take the data and the pictures.

We returned to the hotel and left Moscow the next morning. We flew into Paris, and from there, I left for Torino, Italy to fly a Harrier, while Paul went home. He took the data with him. I spent four days flying an Italian Harrier before returning home for the debriefings.

It was interesting that in the debriefings, several things were kept under wraps. The Russians looked at whether we wanted to become involved in their aerospace industry. It was decided that we did not. One of the things they were trying to sell us was the ejection seats, which were too heavy. But one thing that was noteworthy was that the ejection seats were automatic, especially in their YAK38. If a pilot had a certain degree of nose drop, the seat would automatically eject the pilot. If there was a yaw rate of around thirty-five to forty degrees per second, there was an automatic ejection. This was because the two engines that faced vertically in the airplane were not reliable. They had lost some pilots and aircraft as a result of the engine failures in the hover. We chose not to go with any of their aerospace companies. We believed our technology was as good or better. I don't know whether some of the agencies within the federal government had restricted it as well.

The impression I came home with was that it opened my eyes to what I thought had been a major military power, but was, in fact, third world. People under Communist rule have no sense of optimism or joy, as is common in free countries. When we walked down the street, no one smiled; they just glanced up at us. If we smiled and said hello in their native language, only then would they smile and say hello.

This is one of the biggest differences between America, a nation founded on Biblical principles, valuing human life and freedom as God intended, and a Godless nation. My observations during my trip to

Russia, are also mirrored by missionaries I've spoken with who have served in countries that either are or were under Communist rule. There seems to be a type of national depression that looms over people living in a country where the government oppresses its people and robs them of the freedom that God created them to enjoy. When human beings live under the yoke of Communism, they are suppressed and denied the most fundamental of inalienable rights. They emanate an absence of joy, but more than that, there is an absence of hope. Without hope, there is great poverty, not only in the economy but in the human soul.

Having traveled to many different countries and having the opportunity to observe a variety of cultures, I have come to realize that every nation, as they strive to improve, wants to be like we are. If they cannot be like the United States, they want to tear us down. I believe that is what Al Qaeda and other terrorist groups are trying to do. They cannot be like us, so they want to drag us down to their level. We cannot let that happen. We must not let that happen.

Jack in Russia with Russian Chief Pilot

CHAPTER 19

Family Values

By this time, it may seem that my whole world revolved around airplanes. I admit, flying was an important and exciting part of my life, and airplanes were very good to me. But the single most important thing to me was, is, and always will be my relationship with Jesus Christ, my Lord and Savior, followed by my family. Airplanes were my job—a job I dearly loved, but God is my life, and my family is His precious gift to me. Because of what I did for a living, our family life was a little different than some.

In the business world, travel is common. If I wasn't on a commercial airplane, I was flying my own airplane to one destination or another to test. We flew commercial to meetings in Washington, D.C., and many other locations, so I had to spend more time away from my family than I would have liked.

My family life was entirely different from the way I grew up. When I was growing up, my dad left for work early in the morning, and he was home at 5:15 p.m. every evening. He carpooled with three other men who lived nearby, whose jobs were the same as his. My mother had dinner on the table by 5:30 p.m., and the entire family would sit down to dinner, followed by our chores. Even when I had basketball practice, I was always home for dinner. I didn't remain in a farming community, however, and with my job, my family life changed.

The family is the most crucial building block in society. Without the solid foundation that family provides, society will crumble. History has proven this over the millennia.

In my two tours overseas in West Pac, Arleen held our family unit together. It was important to me when I came home, that I ease back into family life. I never returned with the attitude that I was now head of the house again, or that I should be managing the entire household. Arleen would turn over certain responsibilities to me, such as lawn care or car repairs. We worked as a team.

Arleen saw the children off at the bus stop and picked them up at school. I had the opportunity to attend their school functions and band concerts. There is nothing like listening to a children's band perform on a sweltering hot day. I was so proud! It was the best music I'd ever heard because my child was in that band. I was able to attend the concerts and other events for both of my girls.

I watched my son play Little League baseball. I worked with him, practicing his swing, shooting baskets for basketball, or catching a football. Children are on loan from God for such a short period of time. Our window for making a difference in their lives and exerting a positive influence on them before they go on to have their own families is a brief window indeed, and we must make the best use of our time together.

The two summers I traveled, I brought my family with me to California for the entire summer. We had a wonderful opportunity to see the West Coast. We went to Disneyland, and when the St. Louis Cardinals were in town, we watched them play the Dodgers. At that game, we were winning 5-3. The Dodger fans were a lot of fun. We proudly wore our Cardinal hats, which, of course, brought out the competitiveness of the Dodger fans. We were ribbing them, and they were ribbing us right back. It was all good-natured. In the bottom of the ninth inning, someone hit a three-run homer for the Dodgers, and they won 6-5, which resulted in us being teased for being Cards fans.

We toured some of the historic sites in California—Hearst Castle, the Sequoia National Park, and Death Valley. We went skiing on Mammoth Mountain and saw the LaBrea tar pits in the city of Los Angeles. During the day while I was at work, Arleen and the children would swim in the pool.

Although I traveled often, my family went with me as often as possible. They were with me in Memphis when I was the commanding officer of the squadron there.

Our family always attended the Family Open Days at McDonnell Douglas/Boeing. We would look at the airplanes, and I could show them what I was doing, at least up to the point of breaching confidentiality. We spent as much time together as possible as a family, to keep our unit intact. It was important that we ate dinner together at least three times a week. We'd have Sunday dinner, a Monday night meal, and a third meal each week at the table. Sometimes we would have to wait until Jeff came home from football practice. Jacky worked her senior year, and we sometimes had to wait for her. When we were busy, I'd stop and pick up hamburgers, but we would all sit down at the table and talk and laugh.

The family meal is becoming a lost art, and I believe families suffer because of it. Studies have shown that children do better in school and are much less prone to getting in trouble if they have as many family dinners together at the table as possible.

Arleen and I believed it was important for the children to see the way we ran our family; that there were purpose and order, but not without grace and flexibility. The balancing act worked well for us. I was the head of our household, responsible for paying the bills, and ensuring that everyone was safe and secure. If one of the children had a problem that required a father's viewpoint, that was my job. I helped them with their math homework, and Arleen helped with the other subjects. Arleen was beside me, stride for stride. We were true partners in this, the most important endeavor of our lives. We played to each other's strengths and supported each other's weaknesses. When Arleen made a decision, I would not overrule her. It was a dark day in our family if I did! We would discuss issues behind closed doors to find the best resolution, and never fought in front of our children. We had many lively discussions, but we worked together.

The church was central to our lives, and we tried to model worship and service for our children. Arleen taught our girls to be ladies, and to shine as strong, Godly women. I showed my son that real men loved Jesus, and our strength was in Him.

As a father, one of the core principles that worked for me was to never let a child go to bed with tears. Naturally, I had to discipline my children. Nobody gets perfect children, and no children get perfect parents, and we were no exception. Sometimes when I was traveling, I thought I might have to come through the phone lines and wring their necks.

One time, Arleen called to tell me Jeff had broken the bay window in the living room. He was about eleven years old. I told Arleen to put Jeff on the phone. I was furious.

Jeff got on the phone and sheepishly, almost in tears, admitted, "I broke the bay window."

I calmed myself down because Arleen was upset. I asked him how it had happened. He explained he had a bat and was in the yard trying to hit a golf ball. He threw the golf ball up and would swing and miss, and swing and miss. He tried for at least a half hour to hit this ball. Finally, he got mad and gave up. He was walking back to the house, and he threw the ball up. It hit the driveway with one bounce and went right into the bay window of the living room. His explanation got me so tickled, I couldn't stop laughing. I assured Arleen the window would be fixed. We still laugh about that whenever we talk about it.

One year, when Jeff was at church camp, he got the bright idea to take the ketchup packets, put them on the table, and slap them very hard. Not surprisingly, this sent ketchup splattering all over the female counselor sitting across the table from him in the lunch room. For some reason, she did not find this nearly as amusing as he did, and this little stunt landed him in a boatload of trouble.

It's hard work raising children. There were far more temptations facing our children than there were for me, and each succeeding generation is faced with greater challenges than the preceding one. Without the grace of God and the ability to employ tough love when needed, parenting would be an overwhelming and impossible task.

I had been careful to instruct Jeff that when he was on a date, he should go in, meet the parents, and hold the car door open for the young lady. If she chooses to open her own door, that's fine. I told him it was his responsibility to treat her like a lady.

When Jacky was sixteen, she was interested in a boy who wanted to take her out. I was home and wanted to meet him, to ensure that he was clear about what I required in a young man taking my daughter out. On this particular occasion, the young man stayed outside, honking the car horn. Jacky came running down the stairs, and I stopped her at the front door and asked her where she was going.

She said, "My date is here."

I informed her, "Young lady, you're not going out to that car to meet him. You're going upstairs, and he is coming in."

She stomped off, mad at me. I went out to the car and leaned on the door. The teenager rolled down his window. He was dressed in a t-shirt and needed a shave. He seemed like a nice enough young man though.

I asked him, "Can I help you with something?"

He said, "I'm here to pick up Jacky."

I told him, "I'm Jacky's dad. Here's the deal. You will go home and shave and put on a proper shirt. You will come back and ring the doorbell of my home. I will meet you at the door, and then you will come in. Then, my daughter can leave with you."

He sped out of the driveway.

Jacky was upstairs crying. I thought I'd seen the last of him, but to his credit, about forty-five minutes later, he returned, clean-shaven and wearing a golf shirt. He came to the door, rang the doorbell, and did everything I'd asked him to do. He and Jacky left around 7:30 p.m. that evening.

Around 9:30 p.m., Jacky came back through the door and went upstairs without a word.

The next morning, I asked her, "What happened, you didn't stay out long. You didn't go to the movie?"

Jacky looked at me and said, "Daddy, he was just a jerk."

I told her, as well as her sister and brother that they should hide behind me. If they didn't want to do something and felt peer pressure, they should say they have to check with their dad. I told them if I got a call, I would come to get them. I would be the bad guy. All they had to do was let me know. It happened a few times, but not too many. They made wise choices, and I knew they could be trusted.

When Kathy was a senior at Baylor University, she called me at six, one Sunday morning. We had just gotten up, and she said, "Daddy, I'm about twenty miles outside of Waco, Texas, and my car transmission is broken down."

I thought to myself, *Oh, no. I have to get it fixed,* and I didn't know how I would accomplish this. We were at least a twelve-hour drive away.

There was a brief silence, followed by a giggle, and Kathy said, "April Fools!"

Funny child, that one.

When the children were in high school, I made sure I attended the landmark events for each one of them. Kathy was a cheerleader and captain of the team. We went to the state competition for the cheerleading championships.

The kids all went to youth camp, and we had the youth group from church over to our home some Saturday and Sunday evenings. They knew their friends were always welcome in our home.

When my children were young, I forbade them to go to R-rated movies until they were old enough to make that decision for themselves. I believed it was incumbent upon me, while they were still in my home under my rule, that I should not attend an R-rated movie either. There were several I thought I might have liked to see, but I believed it was important not to ask the children to do something I wouldn't do myself. Every night, Arleen and I prayed for each of our children.

When Jacky attended Baylor, she was instrumental in getting dignitaries to come to the school, including the widow of Anwar Sadat, the Egyptian President who was assassinated. I was so proud of her.

All three of my children had beautiful, memorable weddings, but Kathy's wedding was one for the books! Kathy and Erik got engaged in January 1994, after Erik, a fine young man whom Arleen and I loved, came to me and asked for Kathy's hand in marriage. They had their hearts set on getting married over the Fourth of July weekend. I hoped this would not be a problem, and that I would be able to work around it. Every year, I flew the air shows with the Harrier at the

Arch for St. Louis' Fourth of July festivities, one of the largest celebrations in the United States. Not wanting to rain on their parade and dampen the excitement over a Fourth of July wedding, I agreed.

In March, Boeing announced that they wanted me to do the air show on that Saturday, July 2. I tried to explain to them that my daughter was getting married that day, and I couldn't possibly miss her wedding, but the company was unmoved. They said that while the entire air show was exciting, the plane everyone really came to see was the Harrier, so I *had* to fly, wedding or not. Feeling very much between a rock and a hard place, I went home, and Arleen and I put our heads together to see how we could make this work so that everyone was happy.

Boeing proposed that I open and close the show with the Harrier, and that way, Kathy could get married in between the Harrier shows. Frankly, I thought that sounded like about six different kinds of crazy. Kathy's wedding was at two o'clock at the First Baptist Church of Ellisville. Normally, traffic from Ellisville to the Arch would be just under an hour, but with over a million people at the riverfront for the holiday weekend, I was looking at an impossible situation. The Harrier was parked at Parks Airfield on the other side of the Mississippi River, adding even more time to a packed travel schedule.

Someone got the bright idea of hiring a helicopter to fly me from Parks Airfield after the opening show, to Ellisville. After the wedding, we'd use the helicopter to transport Kathy and Erik to Parks so they could spend their wedding night at a fancy downtown hotel. Mozingo Music was located directly across the street from the church, and the Mozingo family happened to be members of our church. They were gracious enough to allow us to rope off their entire parking lot, so the helicopter could safely land and take off. Hmm, I thought. This might actually work.

Harold Hendrick, of KSIV radio station, heard about our plans, and he contacted the *St. Louis Post-Dispatch* with the story. Word spread and soon, the whole church, the bridesmaids, and family members pitched in together to make this crazy idea happen!

The morning of Kathy's wedding Arleen and I rose early, took yellow parking tape to Mozingo's Music store, and roped off the parking lot. Then I left to open the air show, and as soon as the opening was over, I landed and parked the Harrier at Parks Airfield, rushed to the waiting helicopter and was whisked to the church. We barely landed on Mozingo's parking lot, when I dashed out, ran across the four lanes of Clarkson Road in my flight suit to freshen up and change into my tuxedo in the men's room. Dabbing the perspiration from my face and forehead, I looked myself over in the mirror and decided that I did clean up pretty well, after all.

While the bridesmaids and groomsmen were getting ready, a reporter arrived and interviewed Kathy and me. We were cool as cucumbers; I'd certainly been in tougher spots than this, and Kathy simply had faith it was all going to work out. Maybe not so much with Arleen and Jacky, as they scurried around fixing everything that was out of place, and fussing over every minute detail to ensure a picture-perfect wedding. The newswoman, dressed in a bright yellow outfit was in the sanctuary, where the photographer was trying to take photos. It didn't seem like a circus at all...much!

The wedding was beautiful and went off without a hitch. As soon as the reception was over, I dashed back into the men's room, changed back into my flight suit, and, with Kathy and Erik following behind me, we ran back across Clarkson Road to the waiting helicopter.

The bridal party and all of the wedding guests ran behind us, to see us off. Kathy tossed her bouquet, and the three of us took off with all the wedding guests waving goodbye. It was quite a scene! My other son-in-law, David, videoed the entire event, and later, when he showed it, had the music from *Rocky* playing in the background.

Most of the time, I'm nervous and extra cautious when I'm flying the air shows. These shows are difficult from a safety standpoint. The chance that something can go wrong is always present; only in an air show, if something goes wrong, there are crowds of people who could be hurt or killed. The St. Louis Arch Fourth of July festivities draw over a million people to the riverfront, in spite of soaring temperatures, humidity, parking headaches, traffic, and deafening noise. The pressure of knowing that absolutely *nothing* can go wrong can make for a high-stress day. Add to that a wedding on the opposite end of town in between shows, and you might say the day was a little more exciting than normal! However, I had peace within my spirit that could have only come from God. He gave a beautiful bride and her father a special day that was exciting in a very different way!

December 17, 2003, marked the one-hundredth anniversary of Orville and Wilbur Wright's first powered flight in aviation. The Boeing Company wanted to celebrate the occasion and at the same time, honor me. The Harrier line of jets was finishing, so Boeing had me fly my last flight in the Harrier on that same date, and at the same hour, thus adding another event in aviation history.

The news media covered my final flight in the Harrier, as a large crowd gathered to watch on that brisk December morning. My Harrier expertise had come to an end, and as I stood with Arleen by my side, as she had been our entire marriage, our arms wound tightly around each other, a tear escaped and rolled down my cheek as I bade farewell to this chapter of my life.

Jack and Arleen on his last day of flying the Harrier

I cherish my family memories far and away over any of the airplanes I flew. The planes were part of my professional life, but my heart of hearts was always my faith, my wife, my children, and now, my grandchildren.

My eight grandchildren make the world go around! Grandchildren are absolutely wonderful. The things you missed with your own children because of work or distractions in life, you have the opportunity to see in your grandchildren. They say the most unexpected things, too. The very things that would have gotten my children in trouble have somehow become really cute out of the mouths of grandchildren.

When I played sports as a youngster, if I lost, I didn't like it. I liked to win, and I wasn't a good loser. By the next game, I was over it. But as a parent, I would sit in the stands, watching my son play sports, and I would die a thousand deaths. I would attend my girls' dancing recitals or watch them play in the orchestra, or cheer, and my heart would soar. Watching my grandchildren participate in activities, I can't help but encourage them, because I want them to be successful. Everyone loses in sports, they lose in contests, and they don't always get A's in school. I tell them there is only one Super Bowl, or World Series champion, but there's a new game every year, so keep on trying.

With grandchildren, you don't have to worry about all the things you do when you're the parent. You talk, and you laugh. You get together for grandparents' programs and enjoy your new role, while your grown children take care of the tough parts of child rearing. While I believe no children or parents are perfect, I just might believe that my grandchildren are!

All three of our children married wonderful spouses, and their marriages are solid and happy. The greatest blessing in my life is my family.

The entire Jackson family

CHAPTER 20

The Blue Angels

The Blue Angels are the United States Navy's Flight Demonstration Squadron, with aviators from the Navy and Marines. Formed in 1946, it is the second oldest formal flying aerobatic team in the world. Only the French Patrouille de France, formed in 1931, has been in existence longer. The Blue Angels perform at air shows all over the United States, amazing spectators with daring and dangerous feats. They fly in close proximity to each other, never breaking formation. They are a spectacular sight to behold.

The mission of the United States Navy Flight Demonstration Squadron is, *To showcase the pride and professionalism of the United States Navy and Marine Corps by inspiring a culture of excellence and service to country through flight demonstrations and community outreach.* The Blue Angels are the top of the cream of the crop.

In 1998, I was doing an air show in the Harrier Jump Jet at the Spirit of St. Louis Airport, along with the Blue Angels Navy Demo Team. The event lasted four days. The Blue Angels performed their show, which is always outstanding, right after I finished my show.

I assisted in the development of the Blue Angels' flight control systems for their F-18 Hornet. This connection made it special for me to be a part of the air show with them. Their F-18 Hornet is different from the F-18 the rest of the military uses. The stick force per G (force of gravity) is higher for the Blue Angels because they fly in such close formation to each other. The result of a higher stick force is that it's quite a bit heavier, and therefore, harder to pull.

The day after both of our shows had completed, the flight leader of the Blue Angels asked me if I would have a picture taken with their team. I felt honored to do so. It would be a great ending to a thrilling air show. But there was a slight problem. The Blue Angels were wearing their blue flight suits, and I was wearing a blue flight suit as well, so I wanted another color to mark the difference between them and me. I asked Arleen to please run home and pick out another flight suit. I had several from which to choose, and I didn't care which one she brought, as long as it wasn't blue.

She did so and returned with a black flight suit. It was a very hot, humid day, and the temperature was in the high nineties. I changed into the suit so we could get the photograph taken. Black, of course, soaks up the heat. I thought I would melt. The Blue Angels were calm, cool, and collected as we posed together, while I was practically in a puddle of my own making. That day gave me a whole new meaning to the phrase, *Never let them see you sweat.* Fortunately, the photo didn't show how badly I was sweating.

Jack with the Blue Angels

CHAPTER 21

The Political Arena

I've always been interested in the political process. As my attraction to this area grew, I became increasingly involved in many aspects of politics.

As a senior in high school, I took a government class. Our elderly instructor, Mr. Truman, taught us the legislative process and how our nation's government worked. Our class was small, with only twenty students. We were to elect a president of the class and start the governing body process. There was one group larger than our group, so I was in the minority. I decided to run for president of the class. In order to be elected, I needed to get some of the people from the other group to vote for me. I was not altogether successful in obtaining the necessary votes, but I ran anyway and got a couple of votes.

The day our government class held the election, several of the students from the other group were on a field trip and were not present to vote. When the votes were cast, I won.

Unbeknownst to me, Mr. Truman didn't care for me because he thought I was cocky. Imagine. While I was in his class, I was unaware of his less-than-warm feelings for me, and only learned of them after I graduated.

The first day I presided in our practice government class, I learned that nothing is official until you have an adjournment of the first meeting. I called the meeting to order. We made it through the administrative issues. Someone from the opposing party raised their hand to make a motion. I looked up and announced, "Due to the lateness of starting and the end of the school day, this meeting is adjourned." I sounded the gavel. The students from the other side, and especially the instructor, never forgave me, and Mr. Truman tried to have my election overturned behind the scenes because of this technicality. At the first session, if I had not adjourned the meeting, they could have re-opened it to select a new president.

This experience began to whet my appetite for the political process. It also set the stage for me to understand the huge difference between a politician and a statesman. I believed that my instructor was a politician, and I was definitely not going to be like he was. If he didn't want me to be elected, he should have come to me, but either way, he should have congratulated me. This, my earliest experience in the political process, planted the seeds of a magnetic attraction that even now, continues to grow.

In college, I stayed in a dormitory called Cary Hall at Purdue University. Cary Hall had different wings, denominated A, B, C, D, and E, and Northwest, West, and Southwest, totaling eight halls, with each hall having a president, and one dorm president who presided over the entirety of Cary Hall. In my second year, I was elected president of my hall, Cary Hall, C dorm. I attended the meetings and helped with the by-laws, but I didn't have much more involvement than that.

In my senior year, I ran for president of the entire dormitory of Cary Hall. A freshman who had been involved in the process also ran for president. The night of the debate, my opponent attacked me, alleging I lacked experience. He ranted that I had been more involved with athletics than the political process, while he had devoted all of his time to politics. As I considered the speech I was about to make, I realized that he had also unknowingly attacked the current president. He said things had not been done well, and he would do them better. He blathered on, believing that the worse he could make others appear, the better he would look.

Finally, I stood to address the men in Cary Hall. I said that I felt they had given us a tremendous foundation to grow on. I had observed them in their leadership roles and would take the established principles and build upon them. I had my own ideas for improving things. I was careful not to lambast the outgoing president and his team. I won the election.

Being president of the entire men's dorm at Cary Hall was one of the most gratifying things I did in college, but it also came with many responsibilities. I was on the Campus Student Council and met with the Dean of Men and the Dean of Women at various times. I was also an honorary member of various other organizations, such as student councils for the entire body. That was important to me. We would have council meetings with all the dorm presidents in attendance. I thoroughly enjoyed the process and came to understand some of the duties and responsibilities of elected officials.

That year, after basketball season, we conducted a mock convention in the gymnasium with the delegates. The entire student body was eligible to participate, and we had approximately four thousand students take advantage of this opportunity. There were a certain number of delegates from each dorm. We put our platform together. We didn't vote for a candidate in that election, but we learned the process. The exciting part of this introduction to the political process was that it was almost like a contest, with one side winning and one side losing. When I was older, I realized how important the process was in choosing our nation's leaders.

I did not become involved in politics to a large extent during the early years of my service in the Marine Corps. When you wear the uniform, you have to be removed from politics because you are under the command of the president, whether he is a Democrat or a Republican. The president is our commander in chief so those in the military cannot be in a position where we would be at odds with the very person we are under.

However, there are many other ways a member of the military can be involved in the community. I was president of the PTA one year at my children's school and served as chairman of the deacons at my church.

I considered politics more seriously when I left active duty in 1978. When we settled in St. Louis, I got involved. I chose the Republican party because they were not going to raise my taxes; they supported the Second Amendment, a strong military, and free enterprise. These important issues reflected my own positions, and I felt I could continue to serve my country in this venue.

I visited my councilman, Mr. Stewart. He wrote a letter for me and sent me to an organization, the Pachyderm Club, in St. Louis, which I joined. It provided my first grassroots taste of politics. I began voting the first year in which I was eligible.

When I was on active duty during the first Gulf War, I was called back to North Carolina. We were involved in training young students in preparation for war when the war broke out. It was in November and an election year. I was in my bachelor's officer quarters, watching the elections in North Carolina, particularly the race between Senator Jesse Helms and Harvey Gantt. It was a seesaw battle. In the middle of reporting on this campaign, the media broke in and announced that in Missouri, Joan Kelly Horn had beaten Congressman Jack Buechner by fifty-four votes. That was the district in which I lived. My Congressman had lost. I had forgotten to vote because I was preparing to go to war. That was the last time in my life I missed a vote of any kind.

When I returned home, I became involved by attending meetings and seeing how the presidential campaigns were proceeding. I studied judges so I could be an educated voter locally. I understood that if we were to be a country of the people, by the people, and for the people, then the people better get involved.

In 1999, the Second Congressional seat from Missouri became available. Jim Talent, who went on to become a United States Senator, ran for Governor, leaving his seat as a U.S. Congressman vacant. In the beginning, seven candidates began to vie for that position; then two dropped out, leaving five. These candidates held viewpoints on several important issues with which I did not agree. I traveled to Washington, D.C., to the National Republican Headquarters, and gathered all the information I could on running a campaign. I put together my own campaign and ran for U.S. Congress in the Second Congressional District.

This was quite a learning experience; however, I did not win. But I was not discouraged. Becoming a senator, congressman or mayor, is not a job one can choose. It's up to the will of the voters. Life brings one choice after another. I chose to go to Purdue University and therefore, submitted my application. I chose to enlist in the Marines. I chose to go to TPS. I chose to be a test pilot at McDonnell Douglas, but I couldn't choose to be an elected official. The people choose, and if elected, you serve. However, I learned from my defeat. I learned the political process is not pure, and oftentimes, the best person does not get elected. The gentleman who won that seat remains in that seat, so it was time to move on.

In 2002, I ran for State Representative for the 89th District. I won that seat by a landslide of almost eighty-one percent. This campaigning process was entirely different from the federal level, with more time to go door-to-door, and more time to attend social functions such as Lions Clubs, Rotary Clubs, fairs, picnics, and Fourth of July celebrations. I went to our State Capitol in Jefferson City to begin my first term in 2002, as a state representative. This was the first year in the state of Missouri that term limits went into effect. There was a huge turnover. We had one hundred sixty-three state representatives in Missouri, ninety of which were freshmen.

I wanted to be president of the class. I put in my bid and talked to my colleagues. I was honored to be chosen as the president of such a large freshman class, in which the Republicans were the majority. The Speaker of the House was Catherine Hanaway. I was invited to attend the leadership meetings on occasion and learned how the leadership system operated.

In my second term, I ran unopposed. Because no one ran against me, I won the seat.

Jack and Arleen at the victory party for the 2002 election.
The celebration doubled as his birthday party.

Various experiences leave an indelible mark on our lives. Everyone who was alive when President John F. Kennedy was shot remembers where they were and what they were doing. When our country was attacked on 9/11, every American clearly remembers those vivid details and marks that date as a turning point in our nation.

On that beautiful, clear September day, I was sitting in an AV-8B, preparing to take it on its first flight, when the control tower called and said "Taxi back to your ramp, and shut down. We are in DEFCON 1." Chills snaked up my spine. I thought, All of a sudden, we are at war. There are four DEFCON designations, 1 being the most serious national threat. I knew at that moment, we were under attack. I shut my airplane down and got inside in time to watch the screen as the second plane hit the Twin Towers.

When President George W. Bush was running for re-election in 2004, the Bush-Cheney campaign asked me to be the Chairman of the Veterans for Bush in Missouri as well as on the national level. I accepted since I had already won my seat. I was also given the chairmanship of the Veterans Affairs Committee in the Missouri House of Representatives. There was so much to learn and so many things to do.

That year, Arleen and I went to the Republican Convention in New York, which was held at Madison Square Garden. That afternoon, President Bush was to accept the nomination. We were relaxing in our hotel room when I got a phone call telling me I'd been selected to sit on the stage with others when President Bush gave his acceptance speech.

My first reaction was *yeah, right*. I thought it was a practical joke and a pretty good one at that. But this was no joke. I was going to be on stage with the president of the United States at this historical, nationally televised event! I was so honored, I could barely speak.

I had to report four hours early to a special room for a security check and briefing. I was told where to sit on the stage and what the event would be like. I even had the best seat in the place!

Finally, our little group was assembled in our seats in a packed house awaiting President Bush. When he walked onto the stage, the whole place went wild and I stood up and saluted him. He saluted back and proceeded to give his acceptance speech.

When the speech was over, he started to get his wife, to bring her onto the stage. As he approached me, I saluted him again. Once again, he returned the salute, and said to me, "Thank you for your service."

I replied, "Thank you for being my commander in chief."

He answered, "Yes, but you served in combat." He stood where he was, a kind expression on his face.

I felt the awkwardness that comes from silence when you just don't know what you should say next to the president of the most powerful nation on the planet, yet I felt I needed to fill the silence with something profound. Profundity not being my strong suit, I spoke to my president. "Mr. President, will you do me a favor?"

He answered, "Yes?"

"Will you just win this thing?"

He smiled at me and said, "Yes, we will," and left to get Laura, his wife.

This took place in front of over twenty million people and was one of those moments in time where you feel button-popping pride, and absolute humility in one fell swoop. This is one of my most treasured memories.

*Jack at the Republican Convention
on stage with President George W. Bush*

I became convinced that term limits were not a good idea. I believe that if you don't want an elected official to keep his or her job, it's your responsibility to go to the polls and vote them out. Proponents of term limits, however, will argue that not all Americans vote, and therefore, the only way to get a bad politician out of office is to limit the amount of time they can serve. I disagree with this for two reasons: first, if you have a good public servant doing an excellent job, then you cut them out of a job they've earned, robbed the people of someone who is serving them well, and left the people open to choose a candidate who might not work as well. Second, if the American people are too lazy to vote a bad candidate out, then they deserve to be stuck with him or her. If you don't vote, you have no right to complain.

I also served as chairman of the Joint Committee on Terrorism, Bioterrorism, and Homeland Security, a combination of Senate and House members formed to study Homeland Security for the state of Missouri. It was a very busy time. The September 11 attacks changed nearly everything in the United States. My first two years in office, I was still working at Boeing, as the only Harrier pilot, so my workload was akin to insanity. I would take a leave of absence from Monday noon until Thursday evening, then work on Friday, Saturday, Sunday, and half a day on Monday flying jets, as well as ensuring they reached the warriors.

As an elected official, I wore two different hats: one dedicated to campaigning, and the other to legislative responsibilities. Campaigning involves going door-to-door and fundraising, which I find distasteful. The part of campaigning I enjoyed most was meeting people and sharing my views with them, what I intend to do if elected, and where I stand on various issues. Listening to what the people in my district had to say about the issues and how they hoped I could improve their lives, brought me deep satisfaction. Being called honorable or representative meant nothing unless I was honorable and represented my constituents. It was easy to get a big ego if I wasn't careful. I had to be diligent to not believe everything I was told, and risk losing perspective.

I learned after about six weeks of serving in this capacity, that to be effective as a public servant I needed to have a servant's heart. Without that, it's easy to listen to others extol my virtues when their true motivation was to push their own agenda. There were people who laughed at jokes I told that really weren't funny before I was appointed the chairman of committees. Soon, they'll ask for favors, and the distractions of political gain could pull me from my purpose. Cultivating a servant's heart is the key to staying the course, avoiding misplaced pride, and falling into ethical or moral compromise.

The second part of serving as an elected official is participating in legislative activities. It is similar to that of the federal government. The legislation is filed and sent to committees, where it is heard and either passes or fails, depending on the votes. The proposed legislation is debated and discussed, after which it goes to the House floor for debate. If the Majority Floor Leader and the Speaker of the House decide it is an important bill to consider, then it goes to the House floor for debate. A committee chairman wields power over this. He doesn't have to hear a bill, or he can hear a bill and not vote it out of committee. Many useless, senseless bills were filed, just to appease someone in a district somewhere. If this legislation was passed, it could affect the interest of the entire state. As a state representative, it was my responsibility to ensure that the state of Missouri was a great place to live while ensuring that my constituent's concerns were also addressed.

Debate on the House floor was interesting. The protocol must be followed. We couldn't just call someone by their first name; they must be addressed as gentleman or lady from a certain area. Profanity was never allowed, nor is belittling a person. We were required to keep to the subject matter. Eating was never allowed on the House floor during session, although coffee, bottled water or soda was permitted. Proper attire was a suit and tie, or sports coat and tie. The men were never allowed to remove their jackets while on the House floor. Each person must be recognized before they speak. Adherence to formal protocol keeps the proceedings professional.

I am a member of the National Association of Parliamentarians. In order to be a parliamentarian, I studied Roberts Rules of Order and passed an exam showing I understood the correct procedures in running a meeting. At our first meeting in session, we

were going to debate the rules for the session, and
how to put in place the process for passing legislation.
I read the rules and estimated it would take about two
weeks to pass them. Everyone had received a copy in
advance to study. This was my first exposure to the
politics and partisanship in our state. After three and
a half hours of debate on just the rules alone, we had
not even come close to a decision. I was going crazy. I
felt we didn't deserve to receive our pay for that day,
because it was the Democrats vs. the Republicans and
vice versa, arguing, only for the sake of arguing these
rules. I went downstairs to my office, and my legislative assistant told me that this was the usual process
and it would only get worse. Unfortunately, she was
right!

However frustrating, it was a worthwhile system
to get anything accomplished. Coalitions have to be
formed, and the members need to know the concerns
of others. People love to talk about compromise. In
many instances, compromise is the only way to get
anything done for the good of all concerned. When a
compromise can be reached that serves the interest
of the people, then a spirit of cooperation is forged,
which can lead the way for the future. However, there
are some things which can never be compromised.
I couldn't compromise my honesty or integrity. I figured, once you allow your character to be compromised, you may never regain a position of trust. I could
compromise on issues such as not making new roads
in big cities, but building new roads in rural areas, because people are getting hurt on the roads. In return,
we will have a better school system, and the state will
put more money into the large city's school system
because it's bigger and has more children. These are
just some examples of how I learned to work and understand everyone's needs through compromise.

As much as I would have liked the process to be fast and efficient, in reality, it was the constant back and forth which often made bills that were not good, die on the House floor. Often, it made bills that were good, better. But regardless of the outcome, as a servant of the people, it was crucial to maintain personal integrity.

Once a bill passed the House, it would go to the Senate. The Senate's bills would come to the House. We would work them out. Then the bills would go to the governor, and he would either veto them or sign them. The entire process is intriguing. For example, many times, there were as many as twelve hundred pieces of legislation filed for the year, but only one hundred or fewer were actually signed into law. Many were smaller bills with only a small effect. Other bills were large, such as tort reform and workers' compensation reform that created jobs in the state of Missouri.

Our founding fathers knew what they were doing when they developed the three branches. They understood the need for checks and balances. Everyone was equal in representing their constituents. The system worked well, and to be part of it was rewarding.

In 2005, I began to consider running for auditor for the state of Missouri. Running for state auditor, or any statewide office is a twenty-four/seven undertaking. I only took time off on Sunday mornings to attend church, either my own or another, as a visitor. I was thankful I had access to an airplane and could fly myself around the state to visit various people and find supporters.

The first thing I needed to do was to form a staff. I needed a campaign manager, a political director, and volunteers. Unfortunately, it was important that I raise money. Raising money was the most distasteful thing I had to do in my campaigns and on a statewide level, it was even worse. Once I laid out my convictions, and what I stood for if elected, people were more inclined to help financially, go door-to-door, or put up yard signs, all the things that work together in a campaign. It's expensive. I had to be on television and on the radio, and those appearances must be done professionally.

We traveled the state of Missouri with various teams. The whole family was involved in the campaign process. All three of my children spoke for me. Kathy came up from Tennessee, Jeff from Texas, and Jacky was with me the whole time. Arleen stood beside me throughout the entire process.

One evening, we had eleven different dinners! I flew around the state attending five, and my staff covered the other six. That's the type of stamina required.

What I found interesting, were the different types of people I met who were concerned with the country. Some of them vote. Not everyone votes, however, and that bothers me a great deal. Voting is much more than a right or a privilege; it's the responsibility of every American, beginning on their eighteenth birthday. It's shocking that even after 9/11, when the responsibility to vote is more crucial than at any other time in history, the average American can't seem to be bothered to engage in this important civic duty. They fail to realize that they can lose their freedom due to nothing more than sheer apathy. When a candidate runs for office, they only have to be concerned with thirty percent of the population. The vast majority won't take even a few minutes to cast their vote. Thirty percent of the population votes, but one hundred percent of them complain.

The state auditor's race was an ugly primary, with the Republicans causing a nasty division within their own party, as one candidate would turn on another. Five people were running, and while some ran a good race, others shouldn't have run at all because their families urged them not to run. By refusing to bow out, the votes were split, and better-qualified candidates lost who would have won had they had the votes that had been divided.

I enjoyed traveling around the state and meeting people. When I was in the southern part of Missouri, a man walked up to me and announced, "Jackson, I am a Democrat, and I want you to tell me why I should vote for you." He asked me questions about where I stood on abortion, guns, and higher taxes, but nothing that pertained to the auditor's office. I answered him to the best of my ability.

He said, "Those are all good answers, but that's not the reason I am going to vote for you."

Curious, I asked him, "Well, why are you going to vote for me?"

He replied, "Because I like your boots!"

I often wear cowboy boots. When you're away from the Kansas City or St. Louis areas, a lot of people wear cowboy boots. I've worn mine all my life, so I had them on. I never realized they were going to get me a vote, though.

There was an elderly lady who looked up at me from her walker, put my face in her hands, and declared, "I'm going to vote for you because I like your blue eyes."

Certainly, I was happy to get a vote for any reason, but I would prefer knowing my votes were cast by voters who shared my convictions about more serious issues.

Another man told me, "I'll vote for you if you can answer my question. Where do you stand on the death penalty?"

I thought of all the questions he could have asked about running for state auditor, such as how I would manage money, and how I would hold people accountable, but he was concerned about an issue that had nothing to do with the position I was seeking. So, I asked him, "Sir, of all the questions you could have asked me, why did you ask that one?"

He explained, "Because four years ago, I had a child who went on spring break and was murdered." The murderer only got life in prison. That was his hot button. Once you find out what someone's hot button is, you must draw the line and take your stand.

While a great deal of the questions people asked me about my views had nothing at all to do with the responsibilities of a state auditor, I agree that those questions are important to ask, anyway, whether the person is running for dog catcher, school board, or president of the United States. At some point, a person holding a relatively minor position may choose to run for an office of a higher position. Character matters. While a lot of people asked me about their hot-button issues, many of their seemingly irrelevant questions had more to do with character, and where I would stand on issues if I sought a higher office.

We traveled around the state in about eighteen months. One evening, I had been at an event with three other people, which got me more publicity than anything, although at the time I did not appreciate it. We were taking off at night from a small airport in a little twin-engine airplane. Just as I began to lift off and pull the nose up, a deer ran in front of the airplane. The deer hit the nose of the airplane, the left engine slid under the airplane, tearing the left landing gear off, and the plane immediately veered left and went off the runway. As it went off the runway, I shut the engines down to prevent a fire. I did not need a state representative's hat or one for state auditor. I needed my old test pilot's hat. The airplane careened down the hill toward the trees. I couldn't get it turned, then realized I could use the rudder and brake because we were going about a hundred miles per hour. I did that, and it turned. I thought it was going to go back up on the runway, but because it was sloped, the airplane stayed along the side, giving us a very rough ride. All

I had to do was keep the wings level and not drag the wing tip because that would cause the plane to cartwheel. I was able to stay level, and it finally came to rest by a twenty-foot ditch. Thankfully, everyone on board was unharmed. I shut down the airplane and turned off the gas.

We covered all ends of the religious spectrum during that exciting ride. My campaign manager, Paul Brown, was sitting next to me. When we hit the deer, he blurted out, "Oh shit!" When we eventually stopped, he was as white as a sheet, and exclaimed, "Praise God!"

Another time, we were returning from the southwest part of the state in a replacement airplane. The weather scope showed a huge line of thunderstorms with potential tornado activity between us and home. Discretion being the better part of valor, we landed in Springfield, Missouri, around 6:30 p.m. This time, there were four of us, and we thought it would be best to get a hotel room. What we didn't know was there were sports tournaments all over the city of Springfield, and no hotel rooms were available. We slept in the airport, where they were evidently much too proud of their air conditioning, and we nearly froze. We drove home the next day because the weather was still too bad to fly, so I had to drive back to Springfield on Monday to pick up the plane.

We attended numerous parades and countless dinners. I was constantly speaking and participating in debates which energized me tremendously. The best part of campaigning was meeting so many people. I was able to hear their concerns and the things they were frustrated with, not only in our state but also in our nation. Campaigning was a valuable experience I wouldn't trade for anything, and I'm grateful the Lord provided the opportunity. Unfortunately, I lost the primary race by one-half of one percent, ending my political career in December 2006.

With the close of my career as a political candidate, I determined to remain active in the future of our nation. As the 2008 Presidential campaign began, I reviewed the candidates from both parties, Republican and Democrat. After examining their stand on the issues, I decided to help Senator John McCain. I was designated to co-chair with Senior Senator Kit Bond, in Missouri, for Senator McCain. It was another opportunity to help shape our nation for the present and for the future.

Once again, I traveled the state, this time on the campaign trail for Senator McCain. I was privileged to meet Senator McCain on several occasions, talk with him and understand his philosophy. I didn't agree with all of his principles, but he was our man, and in spite of our differences, I considered him the most qualified of the candidates to lead America.

It was an honor to stand before mass crowds and speak prior to Senator McCain's introduction. Politics and humor, of course, go hand in hand. One time, we held a big rally in Kansas City, at Union Station. We were walking off together, shoulder to shoulder. Senator McCain turned to me, smiled, and said, "Jack, I understand you think you're a better man than me."

I began to laugh because I knew where he was going with this statement. Standing behind him was his staff from Washington, D.C. I furthered the joke. "Yes, sir, in one respect, I believe I am."

I could tell by the looks on the faces of his staff, that they wondered who I was, thinking I was better than John McCain. I continued, "Yes, sir, I am because I can run faster than you. When I got shot down, I didn't get caught."

We both laughed. It was a memorable time, enjoying the interaction with one of our country's leaders.

John McCain had a fun sense of humor. We shared many things in common. He loved his family, and he loved and served his country.

I met Governor Palin from Alaska. She was the real deal. In this campaign, I learned just how extremely biased the media was in their reporting. I was up close and personal with these candidates, and I clearly heard what they clearly said. But by the time the media finished their editing, in keeping with their own agenda, the finished product was so skewed I wondered why they even bothered to show up in the first place.

As we all know, Senator Obama won the election. Because of that, I stepped back. The office of the president of the United States demands respect from everyone. Americans must continue to stay involved and defend the future of our nation, no matter who is in office. But we must also defend the issues we care about. If we oppose the administration, we must stand up as citizens and make our voices heard.

Whether you are for or against any administration and their policies, stay involved. America has too much at stake for her citizens to sit on the sidelines.

After the election, I took time off to reflect on where I'd been, what I'd accomplished, and where God's plan would lead me in the future. I don't know the answer to that question at this time. I do know that I will be involved wherever the good Lord leads me. It's my heart's desire to make this nation a better place for my children and grandchildren. It's my sincerest hope that you will catch my passion for service.

*Jack as Missouri State Representative with Arleen and
President George Bush at Kennebunkport, Maine*

*Jack giving a speech at one of seven ceremonies at the
Vietnam Veterans Moving Wall*

Jack passing one of several veterans bills as chairman of the Veterans Committee in Jefferson City, Missouri

Jack and Speaker Catherine Hanaway honoring former Marine veteran of World War I, World War II and Korea

CHAPTER 22

Final Thoughts and Personal Convictions

I believe the Pledge of Allegiance is important and that every child and citizen should be able to recite it. Crucial to the pledge is the phrase, *one nation under God*. I believe in that when I say it in the pledge because I have a personal relationship with the Lord. He is my Father, and I am His child. This relationship is my reason for living and the highest calling of my life.

The deep convictions of my faith grew even deeper after I returned home from combat. There's something about knowing that at any moment, you could be standing in front of the God of the universe that brings you into a closer relationship and a deeper faith.

I was raised in a home where every time the church doors opened, we were there. My mother was raised in a dysfunctional home. Her alcoholic father made life miserable for all of them. In spite of being married when they were very young, my parents were people of faith, with a close relationship with the Lord. They taught and modeled their faith to their three sons. Growing up in church was a way of life for us.

When I was twelve years old, the faith I had been taught became real and alive to me, more than I ever believed possible. I was a typical, active boy, playing, running, throwing balls, and learning how to shoot a rifle. Every summer, starting around age five or six, through age twelve, I attended Vacation Bible School. It was a two-week program. My mother taught sometimes, and other times, she would stay home with my brothers.

On the last Friday morning, the pastor who led the Bible school explained how one could have a personal relationship with God, through His Son, Jesus Christ. He showed us what the Bible said in Romans 3:23, that we were all sinners, which meant we had all done things that were wrong and displeasing to God. I didn't need anyone to tell me that! I knew even at twelve years old I had done wrong things. Then he told us that Romans 6:23 said the wages of sin is death, and that death meant a spiritual separation from God. If we died in our sins, the only way we could pay for our sins would be to spend eternity in hell. That didn't sound very good to me. But the good news was coming. The Bible said in Romans 4:5 and Ephesians 2:8-9, that we could not get to heaven by doing good works because good works cannot take away our sin. But God loved us so much, He sent His only Son, Jesus, who was perfect and sinless, to die on a cruel cross to make a total payment for our sin, Romans 5:8; John 3:16; I Peter 2:24, and 3:18, and with our sin being paid for, He offers us eternal life in Heaven if we place our faith in Jesus Christ for our salvation, John 6:39-40, 47; John 10:28-29; John 20:31.

I John 5:12-13 tells us that once we have trusted in Christ alone for salvation, we can *know* that we have eternal life. That was the best news of all! To know that Jesus loved me that much and wanted to have a relationship with me was too good to refuse. I understood then that my parents' faith wouldn't save me—I had to own this faith for myself. I understood that going to church wouldn't save me either. That very day, I placed my trust in the Lord Jesus Christ, and He began to live within me right then and there! The following Sunday, I was baptized.

In the Baptist church we attended, there was a tradition of making a public profession of our faith. However, it isn't necessary to have this open profession to earn your way into Heaven, especially since eternal life is a gift that cannot be earned. Public profession is simply a Baptist tradition. But as a boy, I did not quite understand that and thought I had to go forward to make my public profession official. From the time I made that decision in Bible school on Friday until Sunday, I was miserable, fearing that if I died before Sunday, I would not get into Heaven. I was so afraid, but I did not share this with anyone.

Sunday morning came, and we got through the service. The pastor of the church, Gaylord Hamilton, gave the altar call. I shot down the aisle with about ten others. We were all taken into the pastor's conference room. I stood there trembling and told the pastor I didn't understand how this could be so simple.

Pastor Hamilton explained it to me on my level. "My father never broke his word to me. If your dad said to you that he'd bring you a present, you know he'll do that."

"Sure," I answered. "If my dad says it, it's good."

Pastor continued, "I want to ask you something. If you trust your earthly father's promise, how much more can you trust your Heavenly Father's promise? It's a gift from Him."

It all made sense to me. From then on, I never had any doubts about my salvation and what would happen to me upon my death. I know where I will spend eternity.

This foundation laid in Christ was vital to my survival in Vietnam, where I had to trust Him continually with my life. On several occasions, I heard the dying utter, "God save me, I'm dying." Those pleas urged me to not only live my life as I had been doing but to stand up and be counted. I noticed when I would go to dinner, other Marines quietly bowing their heads to silently speak to their God before they ate. In Vietnam, facing death on a daily basis, God took His rightful place as the Ruler of my heart. I acknowledged that He, and He alone, was my only sustenance, and whatever happened to me, I would never leave the palm of His hand. Above all else, I've tried to convey that to my children.

When I was an adult, I was asked to be a deacon in my church. I have served with gratitude. I'm not perfect. There is sin in my life—that is a struggle all Christians deal with, and that is why I am so grateful that God's forgiveness is always available. But David says, "Delight thyself also in the LORD; and He shall give thee the desires of thine heart. Commit thy way unto the LORD; trust also in Him; and He shall bring it to pass." (Psalms 37:4-5). I haven't always been successful, but I have tried to honor Him. In spite of my imperfections, He has given me the desires of my heart.

My family is healthy. I've never had trouble with any of them. My children are happily married, and we have eight wonderful grandchildren. On Father's Day, they all come and sit with me in church. What a joy and blessing!

We show our faith in our service to others. I learned I was not a very good Sunday school teacher, but there is always something I can do, and so can you. If you have a brother who is sick or injured, you can mow his grass, bring a meal or visit him in the hospital. The expression of our inward faith is through our outward service. God can show us where we can be sensitive to the needs of others. While no human's service is ever perfect, I have been humbled to have served as a deacon, an usher, and a trustee. I also dump Easter eggs out of a helicopter for the children to find the Saturday before Easter. It's a joy to watch the little ones as they scramble to pick up thousands of eggs. I've been active in Bible Study Fellowship and Vacation Bible School and helped with the various ministry banquets and events. However, the most important way a Christ follower can serve is by praying for others. Without prayer first, we run the risk of our service being done in our own power, rather than in the power of God. God blessed me beyond measure when I obeyed, no matter how imperfectly, in this way.

There is no man or woman on the planet who does not have sin in their lives. God and God alone stands ready to forgive those sins. It is my hope and prayer that you will come to Jesus in faith for your salvation. Nothing would bless my heart more than to know I will see you in Heaven.

The only hope for our nation is for us to return to being *one nation under God*. Nothing is more important.

Made in the USA
Columbia, SC
11 October 2018